NANOTECTURE

015   **MICRO**

081   **MINI**

151   **MIDI**

213   **MACRO**

269   **MAXI**

Nanotecture continues an interest in the intimate scale of small structures that has always fascinated me. Works such as Toyo Ito's Tower of the Winds (1986), the Basel Signal Box by Herzog & de Meuron (1994), or ephemeral installations such as Dan Graham's Two-Way Mirror Cylinder inside Cube (1988–91) are all examples that caused me to consider the delight of architecture at a diminutive scale. Such modestly sized works, which are often made from a simple material palette, were an inspiration during my architectural education, capturing my imagination for their complexity and materiality, as well as their ability to make an impact far greater than might be expected from their actual size.

In a similar vein as those earlier inspirational projects, this book presents 300 examples of small built works that illustrate how tiny projects can convey interesting design resolutions – all the more compelling for being made in miniature.

Often, smaller scaled works of architecture, design and art are occupied more intimately and so greater attention is focused on how materials are used in such spaces. With this in mind, the material selection of projects here includes works built from humble wares such as timber, plywood and recycled objects as well as recently developed composites – printed concrete, composting bio-plastics and polylactic acids. Equally, there is delight to be found in the follies made of re-purposed and commonly found objects – from hula hoops, corn cobs, pool noodles and umbrellas, to IKEA bins, cable ties and plastic chairs.

Though small, some of the featured works transform to fulfill more than one purpose: Noun 1. Unavailability by Gartnerfuglen (p.64) for example is designed to convert from an icy fishing shelter in winter to a climbing frame for plants in the summer, while the Basic House by Martin Azúa (p.66) self-inflates from a pocket-sized metalized polyester bag into an insulating refuge when heated. In a similar way, the concertinaed wearable shells known as the Veasyble series by GAIA (p.21) fold open from a striking white bag to form an encompassing screen, providing its wearers with privacy in public places. The projects prove that limited size does not preclude – perhaps it even encourages – the ability to make a built project perform well in more than a single way.

Whether micro or macro, many of the projects in this book are designed to be constructed as efficiently as possible: modular, pre-cast, off-site and pre-printed methods of construction affect the time taken to assemble – or disassemble – the works. Some even draw on diverse international communities to take shape. Project Egg, for example, (p.93) is an amalgam of 4,760 components that were each 3D-printed and donated from contributors around the world and united by the designer to form an ovoid pavilion spanning 5 metres (16½ft) wide.

The restricted palette of tiny buildings also requires a maximized logic: the ability to take fewer materials and work efficiently with them. An example is Nidin, which was designed for use in a typically limited apartment space by the French collective Fabbricabois, and combines a sitting room table, a magazine rack and a home for

pets (p.35). Comparably modest and multifunctional is the Miner's Shelter by Dave Frazee of Broken Arrow Workshop, which adds to, and repurposes, an abandoned miner's shelter on the edge of the Arizona desert to become a place to rest, study and converse (p.62). So, too, this logic of multiple use can be seen in Herzog & de Meuron's Structure I-Cube in Jinhua Park, China (p.248). This cast concrete form of an abstract geometrical pattern invites multiple interpretations: its surfaces are scaled to encourage places on which to play, climb, rest, sit or recline.

Tiny built things frequently convey a sense of freedom to experiment without the weighty responsibility of a large budget or complex functional requirements. There is light-hearted appeal in projects such as The Roof that Goes Up in Smoke by Dutch designers Overtreders W – an illuminated, hot-air canopy powered by a wood-burning stove that doubles as a cooker for the picnickers seated below (p.220); or the Story Tower in Cēsis, Latvia – a miniature library and reading corner perched on a public lawn in Cēsis and shingled with Tetra Pak tiles (p.254). Delight and interest is piqued by the glossy, white polyester Blob vB3 in Belgium that is replete with doors hinging upward like wings, and provides mobile, extra space without the requirement for local planning buraucracy (p.45); likewise, Jeffry's House – a shaggy pavilion in County Donegal, Ireland– is positioned to survey the sea and capture local imagination with its distinctive humped profile (p.251).

As with historic predecessors of these works – the strategically located follies of the English Picturesque landscape tradition that were so carefully aligned on axes – many of the projects in Nanotecture respond closely to their context. In France, the Breath Box capitalizes on its seaside location beside a footpath in La Grande Motte, inviting passers-by to interact with its shimmering, mirrored shingles that appear to inhale and exhale with passing breezes (p.170). The crimson bridge made of 22,000 paper sheets in the English Lakes District arches over a stream and impacts on visitors for its surprising structural might as well as its vibrant red colour

that contrasts with the mossy green landscape (p.34).
In New South Wales, Australia, the Permanent Camping tower has a direct relationship to its dry, isolated environment, which is also prone to bush fires: its protective armour of corrugated iron can be folded down on departure to fend off flames and intruders (p.242).

Similarly, a growing awareness of the impact of buildings on the environment is a consideration for projects included in this book. With the density of urban living increasing throughout the world, there is an equivalent sensibility that leans towards the use of smaller spaces with a reduced ecological footprint. This ideology is integrated into the Tree Hotel complex in Sweden, with its forested hotel rooms, such as The Blue Cone, The Birds Nest and the Mirrored Tree House (pp. 38, 129, 257). All of these rooms are required to impact minimally on the Luleå site and allow guests to engage with the natural environment as directly as possible. Similarly, the Walking House (p.239) was conceived of in Denmark but is capable of ambling to whatever environment its inhabitants desire to be in and seems to recall Henry David Thoreau's observation: 'I have a room all to myself; it is nature.'[1] The writer's transcendental approach to life and his deep connection with nature inspired books such as *Walden: Or, Life in The Woods* of 1854. In turn this ideology is explored In projects such as the Walden pavilion by Nils Holger Moorman in Germany – its rectilinear form houses implements and enough space to dwell simply, outdoors (p.182).

Virginia Woolf famously wrote in *A Room of One's Own* that creative freedom required a place of solitude, and contemplation seems to be the ideal companion for a tiny built thing. The two-storey Spirit Shelter (p.140) conveys this – its integrated areas for sleeping, living, reading, socialising and cooking are neatly enclosed inside a timber envelope and the entire retreat can be relocated wherever the owner wishes. Equally pensive is the lofty tea house in Chino by Terunobu Fujimori, which requires courage and a tall ladder to enter: the reward being expansive views and complete privacy (p.40).

These social preferences for bucolic and migratory behaviour, as an escape from cities by many of those in developed worlds, stands in contrast to the increasing challenges of natural disasters, emergency housing and homelessness that are inflicted on others, often without choice. Having small, efficient dwellings that can be erected with speed helps to address vital challenges for human relief, and are seen in the Abod housing system developed for African communities that can be quickly and inexpensively located singly or in groups (p.85). Similarly prompted by shortage and suffering, the GRID housing system developed by Australian practice Carter Williamson Architects was directly informed by the Banda Aceh tsunami (p.265). Its pre-fabricated, flat-packed design can be transported to disaster areas easily and erected within four hours. Seeking a means to provide privacy and refuge, the 1SQM house was developed by Van Bo Le-Mentzel (p.24). Built from spartan materials and with assembly instructions freely available online, it is meant to encourage accessible privacy for all. Small, transportable buildings can also provide temporary assistance for the urban homeless – a tiny but secure place to create some sense of stability for those with none. Projects such as Wheelly (p.39) or the Urban Nomad series of Instant Housing by Winfried Baumann (p.37) and the I-Gloobox replete with rolling cart and storage bags (p.47) confront and answer the basic human need for shelter and security.

Along with these socially-minded projects, Nanotecture also includes a counterpart of spaces that are playful, fleeting, site-specific and without a programme. The Bucky Bar (p.152), for example, was built from a dome of umbrellas around a lamp post and hosted a bar that lasted just one day, while seasonal buildings such as Winnipeg's Warming Huts on the Assiniboine and Red Rivers promote delight and provide refuge but only endure for the winter. A recent public programme, Winter Stations, to utilize life saving huts on Lake Ontario during slow winter months, is seen in the Snowcone (p.103) and Sling Swing (p.69) and prove how successful and

appreciated small structures can be. The annual Serpentine Pavilion is another testament to the allure of small, temporary and site-specific buildings. Now in its fifteenth year, the building and related events generate public interest, cultural debate and have become a noted showcase for experimental architecture in miniature.

Underpinning all these different areas of interest, the 300 works in Nanotecture are united by their petite size. The book is organized into five chapters of progressively larger works: Micro, Mini, Midi, Macro and Maxi. Though there is some overlap in the quantum of projects, they are arranged according to the relative scale of the works. A human-sized treehouse is paired with a tiny bird box while a wooden mountain for a pug dog sits alongside a billowing pavilion for art events, for instance.

Each project is coded according to the sixty-six construction materials used, lending an extra organizational dimension to this book. Projects are cross-referenced in the materials index, and the index of architects, designers, makers and artists.

Above all, *Nanotecture* is a celebration of the small, the compact, the miniature and the tiny. Its collection of inspiring, surprising and delightful small-scale architecture illustrates that size is no barrier to architectural creativity and includes demountable, portable, transportable, inflatable, systematised and flat-packed structures as well as pavilions, installations, sheds, cabins, pods, capsules, tree houses – and even miniature architecture for cats, dogs and birds.

Rebecca Roke

1 – Thoreau, Henry David. Journal, 3 January
1853 from www.walden.org/Library/
Quotations/Nature

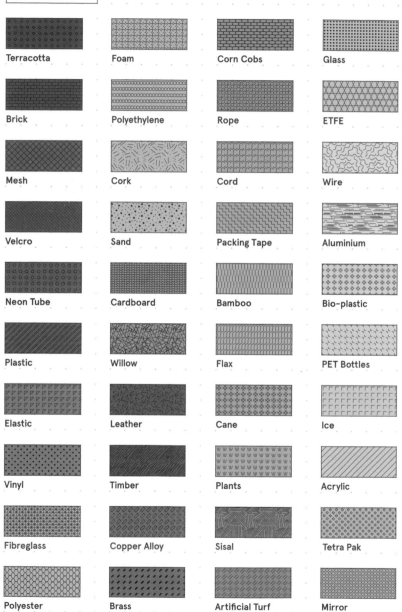

KEY TO MATERIALS

Terracotta

Foam

Corn Cobs

Glass

Brick

Polyethylene

Rope

ETFE

Mesh

Cork

Cord

Wire

Velcro

Sand

Packing Tape

Aluminium

Neon Tube

Cardboard

Bamboo

Bio-plastic

Plastic

Willow

Flax

PET Bottles

Elastic

Leather

Cane

Ice

Vinyl

Timber

Plants

Acrylic

Fibreglass

Copper Alloy

Sisal

Tetra Pak

Polyester

Brass

Artificial Turf

Mirror

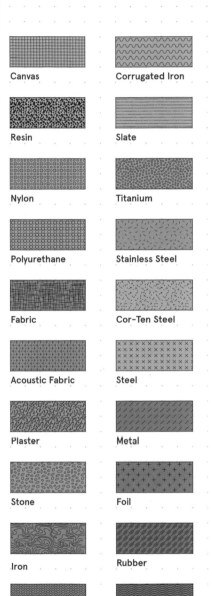

Canvas

Corrugated Iron

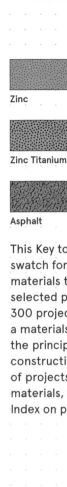

Zinc

Concrete

Resin

Slate

Zinc Titanium

Tissue

Nylon

Titanium

Asphalt

Paper

Polyurethane

Stainless Steel

Fabric

Cor-Ten Steel

Acoustic Fabric

Steel

Plaster

Metal

Stone

Foil

Iron

Rubber

Carbon Fibre

Magnets

This Key to Materials includes a swatch for the sixty-six building materials that appear in the selected projects. Each of the 300 projects is accompanied by a materials swatch that describes the principle materials used in its construction. For a complete list of projects ordered according to materials, refer to the Materials Index on p.326.

MICRO
MINI
MIDI
MACRO
MAXI

This mobile home by Chinese studio dot Architects, consists of a quilted cube attached to the back of a tricycle. The 2 metre (6½ ft) wide structure is made from spray polyurethane foam (SPF), which was injected into a timber and fabric mould held together with pins and string. The foam expanded as it set, so that when the moulds were removed they revealed a bulbous lightweight structure that is both water-resistant and thermally insulated. Bao House is named for this bubble-like surface as 'bao' means bulge in Mandarin. The architects created the structure for Get It Louder 2012, an exhibition of visual art and design in Beijing, in response to a design brief for a human-powered mobile living space.

Standing just 3 × 3 metres (9 × 9 ft) wide, this temporary hut pays tribute to the isolated existence of the Japanese author and Buddhist priest, Kamo No Chomei, who wrote his celebrated book, *Hōjōki* (*The Ten Foot Square Hut*) in 1212, a chronicle of his isolated experience living in a simple forest hut. Kengo Kuma's contemporary version is a latticed structure of cedar beams, which hold a sandwich of ETFE panels in place with magnets affixed to the beams. The temporary hut was assembled from these three layers of 'soft' materials at Kyoto's Shigamo Shrine – said to be the site of Chomei's home – and easily disassembled into stacks of plastic sheets, magnets and latticework several months later.

Part of the designer, Porky Hefer's ongoing interest in indigenous materials and structures, the Tree-Hung nests are a series of human-scaled woven homes that are designed to be hung outside and emulate the traditional nest building technique of the Weaver Bird. its shape is reminiscent of a rustic Eero Aarnio Bubble Chair, and each nest is woven in collaboration with local specialists and varies in size, accommodating up to four people. Its steel frame is woven with Port Jackson willow or local South African vegetation known as 'fynbos'. Suspended from a tree, its hardy materials will endure the elements but the nests can also be used to create a private retreat indoors.

| Project Name **Sphere Houses** | Location **Vancouver Island, Canada** |
| Architect / Designer **Free Spirit Spheres** | Date **1998** |

Accessed by a wooden staircase that winds around adjacent trees, the Sphere Houses are a series of secluded adult-sized tree houses that are part of a private hotel on Vancouver Island. Borrowing techniques from sailboat construction and rigging, each of the spheres is constructed from local cedar or spruce lengths that wrap the shells. Held aloft by ropes attached to trees from three points on the upper side, and secured by lower points, the spheres span up to 3.2 metres (10½ ft) wide and are designed to sway gently with breezes; their lightweight form weighs up to 500 kilograms (1,100 lbs). Inside, the upholstered circular rooms have small windows to frame forest views, and contain a bed, seating and in some even a small galley kitchen.

| Project Name **Tetra Shed** | Location **UK (or elsewhere)** |
| Architect / Designer **Innovation Imperative** | Date **2012** |

 Inspired by the extra room that a humble garden shed provides, this modular tessellated shed is a sleek, customizable work space, designed by UK-based architects, Innovation Imperative. The polygonal shed creates 10.4 square metres (34 sq ft) of spare space in which to work or rest, and is primarily formed from a configuration of fixed and hinged panels that open to create doors and windows. The design also means the sheds can be used singly or joined in a cluster of interlocking workspaces. Formed of plywood panels with bespoke paint or cladding finishes, each Tetra Shed sits on a raised plinth, and can either be delivered fully assembled or made from flat panels.

| Project Name **Veasyble** | Location **Italy (or elsewhere)** |
| Architect / Designer **GAIA** | Date **2009** |

Exhibited at the 2009 Istanbul Design Week, these wearable shells are designed to transform from an accessory into a privacy screen, providing wearers with the option for increased intimacy in their daily life. Formed of cut and folded paper bonded to polyethylene and fabric, each of the four 'screens' in the series – a visor, ruff, bag and mask – protect different body parts. Though the scales for each object differ, the folding module underpinning each piece is consistent. The works are based on GAIA's observation of increasingly populated home and urban environments, and how our idea of personal space may be altered in response to rising urban densities.

Project Name **Pointed T**	Location **Design Miami, USA (or elsewhere)**
Architect / Designer **Hara Design Institute**	Date **2012**

Designed by the Hara Design Institute – one half of the initiative behind Architecture for Dogs that was exhibited at Design Miami 2012 – the Pointed T is a lightweight house for a Japanese terrier. Unlike other designs for the initiative that required specialty materials for construction, this suspended paper cape is simply cut from a large sheet of stationery, taped along one edge, and affixed to the ceiling. The floating territory for a canine creates an ambiguous house without walls or floors and is somewhat akin to a large paper tepee. Dogs can choose to curl beneath the hovering form or peek at their human habitat through the entry cutout.

| Project Name **Casa Lapiz** | Location **Mexico City, Mexico (or elsewhere)** |
| Architect / Designer **Productora** | Date **2013** |

Inspired by Kenya Hara's project 'Architecture for Dogs' this kennel by Productora was one of ten homes for dogs designed by Mexican offices for Dogchitecture, each of which reinterpreted the basic animal shelter. Productora's four-sided pyramidal home combines the practice's interest in pure geometric forms with the necessary requirements to protect a dog from the sun and rain, and provide a warm bed. Made from MDF board and painted with water-resistant gold coloured polyester, the doghouse not only provides a canine sanctuary but is also intended to be a sculptural form in a garden.

 Containing 1 square metre (3 sq ft) of living space inside the bare bones of a wooden and acrylic structure – and taking just one day to assemble – this 1SQM shelter by architect Van Bo Le-Mentzel illustrates how simple it can be to create a room of one's own. As a former refugee from Laos, Le-Mentzel's design is an homage to the emotional and physical importance of having your own space. The DIY house encloses a bed, desk, light and operable window, and can stand upright like an office or booth, or reclined for relaxation, depending on the owner's needs. In the same spirit of accessibility, plans and costs to build 1SQM are available to download for free.

Project Name **Beagle House**	Location **Design Miami, USA (or elsewhere)**
Architect / Designer **MVRDV**	Date **2012**

Revising the archetypal form of a dog kennel, this interactive version by MVRDV is one of thirteen works of Architecture for Dogs that were conceived and commissioned by the Hara Design Institute with the Nippon Design Centre for Design Miami. Rather than trotting out a typical straight-sided dog house, the curved walls, floor and ceiling of the Beagle House accommodate the playful and intelligent nature of this breed of dog. Each time he steps into or out of the kennel, it responds in kind with a gentle rocking motion. Unlike other works commissioned for this series, the Beagle House can be used independently from its owner's house. Weighing only 5 kilograms (11 lbs), the Beagle House has a robust rope attached to its base that makes it easy to relocate to wherever dog and owner prefer.

Project Name **Nestbox**	Location **Cardigan, Wales, UK (or elsewhere)**
Architect / Designer **JAM Furniture**	Date **2014**

Recalling a humble milk carton, the sustainable and ecologically responsible designers at JAM have created a chic birdhouse that is predominantly made from recycled materials. Off-cuts from local manufacturers form the front and rear of the house, which are wrapped by riveted sheets of re-painted metal sourced from discarded washing machine and dishwasher bodies. To accommodate various different species of birds, the entry holes of the Nestboxes are cut to four variable sizes and all roosts are made of knurled brass rods that allow birds to grip their perch easily.

| Project Name | **Bird Apartment** | | Location | **Komoro City, Japan** |
| Architect / Designer | **Nendo** | | Date | **2012** |

Designed by Nendo for the Ando Momofuku Center in Japan's
Nagano Prefecture, this gigantic birdhouse provides spaces for
seventy-eight bird nests but also allows humans a glimpse into
how birds live. Positioned high in a tree and accessed by a ladder, visitors can ascend to
the box and enter through a human-sized entry that mimics a traditional bird box. Within
this sheltered space, one-way viewing holes are set into each nest to provide unobtrusive
avian viewing. The opposite side of the birdhouse is peppered with dozens of holes for
birds to enter through, each painted in shades of white and greys.

| Project Name **Mirror House** | Location **Isle of Tyree, Scotland, UK** |
| Artist / Designer **Ekkehard Altenburger** | Date **1996** |

This temporary installation by sculptor Ekkehard Altenburger appears as a mirrored house that floats on the water in the Isle of Tyree, Scotland. The structure of mirror and steel frame typifies the shape of a small house and rises to a 2 metre (6¾ ft) high pitch, reflecting the surrounding sky, water, rock and heather. Its 1.5 metre (4¾ ft) wide facades blur the boundary between what is real and what is reflected, creating a changing scenography of natural elements. Like much of Alternburger's work, the Mirror House explores a balance between the built and natural environment and how our perception of these can be manipulated.

The Lookout was designed and built during the final year of Angus Ritchie and Daniel Tyler's architectural studies, funded by the government for a programme organized by the Scottish Scenic Routes Initiative. This timber-framed, mirrored cabin sits in the Loch Lomond and Trossachs National Park and reflects the spectacular landscape of its lochs, rivers and burns. Clad in sheets of polished stainless steel, and framed by exposed plywood edges, it multiplies and contrasts views of the water, sky and hills. A slatted timber bench for two is set into the rectilinear structure, protected by a small overhang and providing a place to sit and contemplate.

| Project Name **Bicycle Sauna** | Location **Czech Republic (or elsewhere)** |
| Architect / Designer **H3T Architects** | Date **2011** |

Designed to be towed by a tandem bicycle, this novel transportable sauna is imagined as a lightweight place in which people can socialize while engaging with their changing surroundings. Made of translucent polycarbonate panels bolted to a cylindrical timber frame and braced across an axle, the sauna can squeeze up to six people on the wooden benches inside. Entry to the pod is via a slice in the elastic membrane that seals in heat generated from an efficient internal fireplace. The only giveaway of the function inside H3T's prototype for portable architecture is smoke rising from the diminutive chimney housed inside a green fabric cover.

| Project Name **Roaming Market** | Location **London, England, UK (or elsewhere)** |
| Architect / Designer **Aberrant Architecture** | Date **2013** |

Commissioned as part of the Mayor of London's Waterloo Portas Pilots project, this roaming folly is based on the city's historic street markets and Lambeth borough's colourful history of fortune tellers and mystics. The movable venue of blue-painted steel holds a covered seating area for chess and fortune readings, and a rooftop plinth for installations and events. A totemic chicken signpost that references the Roman's use of fowl to predict the future crowns the Roaming Market, which can move to various locations along Lower Marsh and The Cut, providing a playful attraction in the area. Mounted on a trailer chassis, its collapsible steel balustrades mean the stall can be lowered in height and easily stored.

Project Name **Blocks**		Location **USA (or elsewhere)**
Architect / Designer **Poopy Cat**		Date **2014**

Borrowing from children's playful approach to building blocks, this modular set of cardboard beams, cubes, tunnels, bridges and ramps is designed as a transformable playhouse for cats. Made from white-coated recycled card and punched with decorative graphics and cat-sized holes, each of the playhouse elements can be simply slotted together with card tabs, which also secure the stacked blocks. The set of blocks can be flat-packed and is light enough to be carried in a large portfolio case yet strong enough to bear the weight of several cats.

Suspended between trees at the edge of a forest clearing in Dorset, this adult-sized cocoon was created by students of the Architectural Association School of Architecture using just four sheets of untreated plywood and a milled local cedar tree. Having determined the best location and height to mount the cocoon in order to take in winter sunsets within the park, the design was prefabricated off site. Its timber skeleton was bandaged by lengths of green wood, which provided structural stiffness once dry. Designed to weave precisely around the three trees from which it hangs, the cocoon is entered by a small staircase, which leads to the wrapped interior that is big enough to sit in and faces an aperture from which to observe sundown.

Project Name **Paper Bridge**	Location **Cumbria, England, UK**
Artist / Designer **Steve Messam**	Date **2015**

This striking bridge was designed by artist Steve Messam, as part of the Lakes Ignite Cultural Festival. Made from 22,000 sheets of red paper, it stands in marked contrast to the burnished and stony hues of the Lake District's Grisedale Valley. The crimson bridge is held together with neither glue, bolts or other adhesives. Instead, the self-supporting bridge draws on age-old structural principles of dry stone walls; here the angled paper is wedged together between gabion cages to form a low arch in a similar style to traditional English packhorse bridges. Able to support the weight of a person, *Paper Bridge* was eventually dismantled and fully recycled in accordance with Messam's environmental intent.

Project Name **Nidin**	Location **Paris, France (or elsewhere)**
Architect / Designer **Fabbricabois**	Date **2015**

Combining an animal shelter, magazine rack and low table, the Nidin is designed by French studio, Fabbricabois and fulfills all three needs with a single piece of furniture. Made from triangular, square and rectangular sheets of birch plywood, the multifunctional piece is based on the Japanese concept of origami. In this instance, the folded paper sheets were revised to become cut and chamfered niches that allow the six components to fit together without nails, screws or glue. Careful incisions in the table top and base are angled to accept the walls of the animal shelter and magazine rack while large elastic bands mounted into the base fit over the lateral sides of the table top and secure the assemblage.

 Part of a benefit hosted by Architects for Animals to raise funds for LA-based cat charity, FixNation, DSH Architecture's Cat's Cradle was one of several designs contributed by notable local architects for bespoke feline housing. The shelter is made from five intersecting aluminium hoops that are arranged in a dynamic form – three of them provide a gravity structure while the other two are wrapped with rayon cord that creates a webbing platform and sunshade. Appropriate to the Californian climate, the project is imagined as a place for cats to perch on and observe from, its taut strings providing a playful feline diversion as well as dappled shade.

Project Name **Instant Housing**		Location **Germany (or elsewhere)**
Architect / Designer **Winfried Baumann**		Date **2001**

In recognition of the difficulty in providing secure, vital shelter for urban nomads, disaster situations and for the homeless, Winfried Baumann created the Urban Nomad series – a range of lightweight and transportable housing. Each of the mobile homes accommodates one person and is equipped with emergency supplies, including a first aid kit, torch, whistle and retractable padded bed. Easily manoeuvred alone, the homes provide the basic necessities of shelter, aid, light and warmth. This iteration of the Urban Nomad includes a steel shell mounted on bicycle wheels and is supported by three pairs of legs. As with each house, the structure is enclosed by a demountable nylon or plastic hood.

Project Name **Blue Cone**	Location **Luleå, Sweden**
Architect / Designer **SandellSandberg**	Date **2010**

Anchored above rocky terrain, this cabin mimics a classic gabled house profile in miniature but is distinguished from traditional wooden chalets by its red-coloured birch shingle cladding. Visitors enter via a red ramp that leads through a forest grove to wheelchair accessible accommodation, part of the Tree Hotel complex. Though only 22 square metres (72 sq ft), the interior of the eccentrically named Blue Cone includes four beds, a living room and bathroom. In contrast to the bright exterior it is lined with timber flooring and white-painted walls, which accentuate its pitched height. The focus of the cottage is a large picture window, which frames unobstructed views to the Harads landscape.

 A solution to the basic human need for shelter, the Wheelly was designed by Italian studio, ZO_loft, as a portable and protective home for those without one. The house centres on a large aluminium wheel that stands 150 × 4 centimetres (59 × 1½ in) wide, flanked by two collapsible polyester resin tent tubes that are affixed to each side. The nomadic home can coast through the city with roller-bearing technology and is manoeuvered with a sturdy aluminium handle, which becomes a brake once the wheel is set down. Dwellers enter via a retractable opening in one of the colourful tent tubes; the other end is secured by a rubber seal that can be used to display messages or sponsorship logos, allowing the users to offset the cost of their accommodation.

 This tea house was built and designed for Terunobu Fujimori's own use and sits atop two chestnut trees, which were harvested from a mountain nearby and form the support for this shingled folly. Accessed by free-standing ladders, the tea house is clad with plaster and charcoaled shingle roof tiles, with a simple interior of white-painted walls and tatami mats. Measuring less than 3 square metres (9¾ sq ft) inside, there is enough room to prepare tea over a fire and sit in contemplation. The precarious height of the project allows distant views to the town of Chino – a framed living landscape that replaces the traditional picture scroll which is usually hung in tea houses.

| Project Name **Nestrest** | Location **Germany (or elsewhere)** |
| Architect / Designer **Dedon** | Date **2010** |

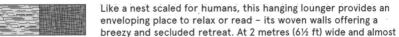

Like a nest scaled for humans, this hanging lounger provides an enveloping place to relax or read – its woven walls offering a breezy and secluded retreat. At 2 metres (6½ ft) wide and almost 3 metres (9¾ ft) tall, the lounger mimics the sophisticated interleaved design of many bird's nests in technique and hue. Easily suspended from a tree branch or other sturdy support by its system of ropes, the Nestrest is light enough to sway with the breeze – just like an avian abode. But in contrast to twigs and leaves built by birds, this project has an altogether more luxurious interior with a large mattress cushion and finishes of leather or cloth.

| Project Name **Tree House** | Location **Ljubljana, Slovenia (or elsewhere)** |
| Architect / Designer **Robert Potokar and Janez Brežnik** | Date **2008** |

In contrast to ordinary tree houses that are embedded within supportive tree branches, this self-supporting version is designed to stand *beside* a tree – providing the experience of treetop dwelling without relying on the necessity of a tree's strength or form. Constructed of spruce plywood and roofing cardboard, the house is accessed by a ladder, which leads to the 3.5 square metre (11½ sq ft) interior. Inside, the main focus is a large acrylic picture window, which frames the landscape. Simple built-in benches secured with dowel pins, and operable windows at different heights create an interactive play experience.

Project Name **Organic Cube**	Location **Copenhagen, Denmark**
Architect / Designer **Søren Korsgaard**	Date **2009**

Built in the gardens of the Statens Museum For Kunst, this temporary timber pavilion celebrates the sculptural and structural potential of wood and was constructed for Copenhagen's International Wood Festival in 2009. Shaped from a grid of long laths cut to identical dimensions, the perception of the cube changes as one moves around it. From one side it looks to be a strict wooden lattice but this appearance gradually dissolves, becoming more open to reveal a parabolic arc within. This twisting effect is created by rotating and displacing the internal laths from the grid; as well as illustrating the potential of laths, they cross-brace the pavilion and create two spaces for children to play in and climb on.

Project Name **Cristal Bubble**	Location **France (or elsewhere)**
Architect / Designer **Pierre Stéphane Dumas**	Date **2014**

One of a series of unusual transparent, inflatable hotels, the Cristal Bubble is intended to replicate the pleasure of sleeping under stars without sacrificing the comfort of shelter, bedding and other everyday luxuries. Developed by Pierre Stephane Dumas and available to rent in Bubble Lodges throughout France, Spain and Switzerland, the Cristal Bubble is the most simple version of six bubble designs, each inflated by a noiseless ventilation system that filters air, prevents humidity and retains the spherical shape without framing or other structural support. Easily dismounted and reassembled, the experience of camping in a Bubble Lodge is readily changed, shaped each time by different surroundings.

Commissioned by XFactorAgencies to make an extension for their office, dmvA developed the Blob – a sustainable, low-energy extension that would defeat strict building codes and provide extra mobile space in the highly populated region of Flanders. Providing a 20 square metre (65¾ sq ft) insulated, weatherproof room, the Blob contains a kitchen, bathroom and bed, as well as numerous integrated niches to store possessions. Its glossy white form is like an enormous cocoon that is incised by a hinged door, a small cupola skylight and a nose that opens upwards to create a sheltered veranda below. Small enough to be transported on the back of a truck, the body of the project is made from a timber frame and enclosed with multiple layers of smoothly-finished polyester inside and out.

Project Name **Cardborigami**	Location **California, USA (or elsewhere)**
Architect / Designer **Tina Hovsepian**	Date **2007**

Tina Hovsepian designed the Cardborigami in a bid to alleviate the situation of homeless people in her native city of Los Angeles. These temporary shelters are formed of treated cardboard and use the folding principles of origami to create an expandable, stable and private home for those without one. The Cardborigami shelters are part of Hovsepian's larger campaign to address chronic homelessness and are designed to be water resistant and flame-retardant. Manufactured locally, Hovsepian's shelters can be quickly assembled by two people. The cardboard shells can also be customized by owners to create a sense of personal identity; when damaged beyond use, each shelter is fully recyclable.

Project Name **I-Gloobox**		Location **Bulgaria (or elsewhere)**
Architect / Designer **Georgi Djongarski**		Date **2006**

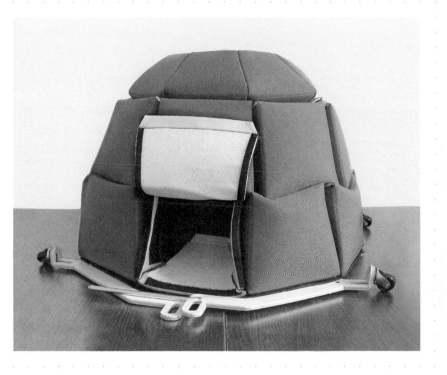

Designed to provide basic needs for the homeless, the I-Gloobox was developed by Bulgarian designer Georgi Djongarski and serves as a practical, moveable and insulating temporary home. The shelter mimics the form of a conventional igloo but instead of ice, each brick is formed from individual panels of foam-filled fabric that also carry storage pouches on the inside. Unfolded, the I-Gloobox stands as an isolated dome-shaped pod framed by aluminium legs with a padded bedroll and an entry that can be secured. Packed up, it transforms into a wheeled cart, replete with saddlebags – the design making it easy and light to move.

| Project Name **Attic** | | Location **USA (or elsewhere)** | |
| Architect / Designer **Studio Chad Wright** | | | Date **2011** |

Establishing a different sort of pecking order, these elongated archetypal birdhouses by Chad Wright offer a playful alternative to traditional wooden nesting boxes. The brightly painted timber pillars of tomato red, robin's egg blue and cloud white are available in various heights from 1.4 metres (4¾ ft) to 1.8 metres (5¾ ft) tall. Each of the slender columns is stabilized by a stake screwed into its concrete base, which allows them to stand securely on tiles or lawns. A simple dowel perch and faux chimney complete the ensemble for these avian penthouses.

 Standing somewhere between sculpture and architecture this shaggy black folly is part of the Brick Bay Sculpture Trail in Matakana, New Zealand. The 12 metre (39½ ft) high tower is clad in curling shingles of oversized tyre treads, which gives the habitable structure its hairy appearance. Though the folly's name suggests brutish references, its form is designed to be deliberately ambiguous and could equally allude to traditional *Kahu tōī* (Maori flax cloaks). Providing a diversion for visitors to the trail, Belly of the Beast is also intended as a sustainable endeavour: once its twelve-month residency is complete, the structure will be disassembled and recycled into rubber chips for use in equestrian arenas.

Project Name **Scale In-between**		Location **Stockholm, Sweden (or elsewhere)**
Architect / Designer **Worapong Manupipatpong**		Date **2007**

This structure is one of several timber pavilions designed by Worapong Manupipatpong that explore the small scale of objects that fit neither traditional categories of furniture nor architecture but can be used by adults to sit on, read in, climb up or look out from. Fascinated by the quality of 'smallness' yet scaled for adults to fit in, each of the pine pavilions is imbued with the nostalgia of secret cubbyholes and huts for children to play in. Like a room without furniture, the different spaces encourage grown-ups to recline or hide away and can be used to make semi-private spaces in parks or public places.

| Project Name **BuBble** | Location **Mexico (or elsewhere)** |
| Architect / Designer **Studio MMASA with Cipriano Chas** | Date **2009** |

 Designed by Patricia Muñiz and Luciano G. Alfaya, with Cipriano Chas, the BuBble was envisaged as a temporary form of accommodation for transient people or those displaced from their homes. Enclosed by four walls of inflated transparent plastic, the nomadic skinned structure is supported by a demountable tubular aluminium frame, with an operable wall/ door that hinges open to allow entry, as well as creating a protective canopy. In order to meet the minimum needs for human hygiene and comfort, the BuBble also includes a water point and single gas hob. The entire unit – including cooking equipment and folding camping stool – packs down into a single box that allows for ease of transportation.

| Project Name **Roomoon** | Location **Devon, England, UK (or elsewhere)** |
| Architect / Designer **The Hanging Tent Company** | Date **2014** |

 Providing a respite from the typically mired fields of English festival campsites, the Roomoon was designed as a portable hanging tent that could float high above the mud. Its spherical form is made of six structural ribs, spanned by a canvas skin, with a 1.8 metre (5¾ ft) wide circular floor, which can be rolled up and transported by car. Coats and muddy wellington boots can be stowed in the undercroft, leaving a clean platform that comfortably sleeps two people. Each Roomoon can be assembled in less than an hour and suspended up to 3 metres (9¾ ft) in the air from the continuous zinc-plated chain.

| Project Name **TreeTents** | | Location **The Netherlands (or elsewhere)** |
| Architect / Designer **Studio Dré Wapenaar** | | Date **1998** |

Designed by Rotterdam-based sculptor and tent-builder, Dré Wapenaar, the TreeTent originally arose from his desire to make shelters that could hang from trees and provide protection for environmental activists. The globular tents are made of a steel frame wrapped in canvas and span almost 3 metres (9¾ ft) wide, tapering upwards from the circular base, which provides a sleeping platform for a family of four. The teardrop shaped geometry of the tents is the result of natural laws of gravity. Inside, each of these portable, sculpted 'buildings' holds a large circular mattress and each is available for holiday rental at the Hertshoorn campground in the Netherlands.

| Project Name **Antoine** | Location **Verbier, Switzerland** |
| Architect / Designer **Bureau A** | Date **2014** |

Commissioned by the Verbier 3D Sculpture Park Residency, this wooden cabin is camouflaged inside an artificial rock that hangs on a rock fall field in the Swiss Alps. Imbued with the spirit of adventure often sought in the Alps – a place for observation, dwelling and hiding – the cabin is designed for a single occupant. Its knobbly rocky facade disguises a simple refuge in which to sleep, eat and contemplate. Named for the shepherd, Antoine, in Charles-Ferdinand Ramuz' novel, *Deborance*, who survives for seven weeks in a rocky landslide, the cabin was built by hand in a mountain village and transported to the site on the back of a truck. Perched in its precarious location, the small window and narrow door are the only external clues to what lies within.

Surrounded by lichen-coated granite outcrops and overlooking the waters of an inland pond in Deep Bay, this, the fourth artist's studio for the Fogo Island Arts Corporation is an isolated retreat. Referencing a traditional Newfoundland fishing 'stage', from the island, the studio appears to be a timber parallelogram without windows. Propped up by four piers, its cantilevered bulk is connected to the granite by a bridge and on approach, a large glazed entry leads to the 130 square metre (1614½ sq ft) space. The sloping building is divided into two levels: a large picture window frames the workspace on the upper tier, with a small kitchen and wood-burning stove below. Ceiling, floor and walls are all clad with white-painted spruce planks that echo the perspectival slant of the rooms.

Looking to find a solution to counteract the shrinking bird population in urban areas, craftsman Klass Kuiken consulted with the Vogelbescherming (Dutch Bird Association) to design the Birdhouse Rooftile. Birds often create nesting areas within the roofs of houses, and the Dutch designer took this into consideration, adapting a standard roof tile to include an archetypal bird box on top of it. Birds access the house through an opening that leads to a basket for sheltered nesting below. A comb-like barrier placed directly beneath the roof tile ensures that birds are unable to access the main roof space and makes the house easy to clean once breeding season is over.

| Project Name **Cricklewood Town Square** | Location **London, England, UK** |
| Architect / Designer **Spacemakers** | Date **2013** |

This mobile town square was designed for the community of Cricklewood in north London in response to the absence of civic amenity in the area, which currently has no town hall, no library, no public plaza nor a park bench. Marked by a portable miniature clock tower mounted on a rickshaw bicycle, the tower contains the necessary components to complete a town square, including benches, stools, umbrellas and signage in the form of a diminutive civic folly. Installed at various locations around the area and constructed by Studio Keiren Jones, the project was intended to illustrate the importance of public space and highlight this overlooked civic resource.

Project Name **TuboHotel**	Location **Tepoztlán, Mexico**
Architect / Designer **T3arc**	Date **2010**

 This Mexican hotel offers tourists an eco-friendly experience with rooms made out of recycled industrial concrete storm drains and sewers. Located outside the village of Tepoztlán, about one hour's drive from Mexico City, the twenty tubes on offer at the TuboHotel come fitted with a queen-sized bed, and a mountain view through the glass door. Designed as backpacking and hostel accommodation, the TuboHotel has welcomed many different campers because of its unusual design. Guests can stay in their concrete cots for around US $40 per night and though the facilities are basic, each tube includes a bed, a night lamp, fan and storage space.

Project Name **Sledge Project**	Location **Uummanatsiaq, Greenland**
Artist / Designer **Rob Sweere**	Date **2009**

Commissioned by the Uummannaq Polar Institute and Ann Andreassen, these two habitable sleds by Rob Sweere are temporarily parked in the landscape of Uummannaq Island in Greenland, north of the Arctic Circle, overlooking spectacular ice floes. Built with the assistance of Inuit hunters, the two white wooden buildings can accommodate up to six people and are fully insulated. Fitted with a table and wooden benches, they are designed to allow visitors to sleep, cook and rest in the striking environment and are light enough to be towed by draught horse across the sea ice.

| Project Name **Kekkilä Green Shed** | Location **Helsinki, Finland (or elsewhere)** |
| Architect / Designer **Hel Yes!** | Date **2010** |

 Situated on a remote island in Finland, this combined green house and storage shed is one of four variations designed by architect Ville Hara and designer Linda Bergroth of Hel Yes! The design accommodates living, sleeping, reading or dining in the large glazed area with a secure wooden shed behind in which to store tools and supplies. Made of Finnish pine and toughened safety glass with automatic controls for the internal temperature, each glasshouse is supplied in ready-made elements that are intended for self-assembly on site, requiring only a screwdriver. In this instance, Bergroth customized her standard prototype glasshouse by adding a wooden floor in the main space, solar panels for lighting, and reclaimed brick steps to the neatly organized rear shed.

| Project Name **Lègologica** | Location **Rome, Italy (or elsewhere)** | Date **2011** |

Architect / Designer **Francesco Bombardi, Andrea Bergianti, Simone Ardigò**

 Designed as a one-to-one scale prototype for a zero energy home, the Lègologica house is based on the simple accretion of blocks that resemble the popular children's construction toy, Lego, for which the house is named. Unlike the solid play blocks, these hollow, light bricks are bounded by a wire mesh that can be filled with indigenous materials found near to a chosen site, such as rocks, stones, earth or even pine cones. Providing insulating properties and requiring almost no transportation, the found building materials encourage thoughtful use of local resources. Timber-framed windows can be punched into any facade, depending on the preferred aspect and sun orientation, and each house has a half-gabled roof that is clad with solar panels.

Project Name **Miner's Shelter**	Location **Taliesin West, Arizona, USA**
Architect / Designer **David Frazee/Broken Arrow Workshop**	Date **2011**

 Re-occupying a disused 1980s copper miner's shelter in the Arizona desert, this tiny dwelling was designed and built by David Frazee while studying at the Frank Lloyd Wright School of Architecture in Taliesin West. Built above the existing low concrete boundary wall and designed to face the original functioning concrete chimney stack, the exterior cladding is of oxidized steel panels and ebony-stained redwood, which blends in with the rich desert hues of rust and sand. The L-shaped building is just large enough to accommodate a single bed and has views to the desert from the full-height windows and a glazed door. Lined with plaster and pale birch plywood the only additional interior comfort is an in-built ledge for displaying small objects.

Project Name **Cat Cube**	Location **Los Angeles, California, USA (or elsewhere)**
Architect / Designer **Standard Architecture and Design**	Date **2014**

 A series of cat houses designed by Los Angeles-based architects were created for the 'Giving Shelter' fundraiser organized by Architects for the Animals. More than twelve local architecture practices created structures for a one-night-only exhibition and cocktail event that raised money for the animal charity FixNation. This Californian organization is dedicated to humanely controlling feline populations by catching, neutering and returning the animals to where they were found. The Cat Shelter by Standard Architecture and Design is mainly formed of cast concrete, which frames a cube housing timber platforms and a protruding timber viewing platform at the rear.

This small ice fishing shelter is a portable, timber-framed structure on the edge of Lake Møsvatn, that can be easily assembled and built with, and alongside, nature. Its walls of chicken wire are filled with panels of ice formed from lake water nearby, which creates a barrier against winter wind and diffuses sharp sunlight. In winter, the icy facade blends with the snowy environment and its candlelit interior casts a gentle glow when the sun sets. During summer, the shelter transforms to become a gazebo on which to grow edible climbing plants, such as peas, beans or cucumbers. Similar to the natural effect of the wintery ice panels, the plants provide shade and shelter from the elements.

| Project Name **Manifest Destiny!** | Location **San Francisco, California, USA** |
| Architect / Designer **Mark Reigelman and Jenny Chapman** | Date **2012** |

 A collaboration between artist, Mark Reigelman and architect, Jenny Chapman, this tiny suspended cabin clings to the side of the Hotel des Arts in San Francisco, and is intended to emphasize the right to seek out and inhabit unused space in urban environments. Constructed from a welded aluminium frame clad with 100-year-old reclaimed timber planks, the cabin stands just 3.5 metres (11½ ft) tall and is punctuated by small rustic windows, shrouded by curtains, which are lit by night to draw attention to the project. Hanging 12 metres (39½ ft) above the street, *Manifest Destiny!* acts as a throught-provoking and lonely beacon in the middle of busy city streets.

| Project Name **Basic House** | Location **Spain (or elsewhere)** |
| Architect / Designer **Martin Azúa** | Date **2010** |

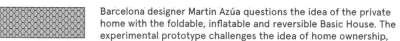 Barcelona designer Martin Azúa questions the idea of the private home with the foldable, inflatable and reversible Basic House. The experimental prototype challenges the idea of home ownership, offering an alternative to the materialistic reality of today's world. Made from metalized polyester that is so light it floats, Basic House is intended as a shelter small enough to fit in your pocket, allowing you to break away from the imprisonment of materials ties. The shelter self-inflates with body heat or from the heat of the sun, protecting users from both the cold and from the heat.

 Entitled Mirror Cloaking, this winning entry in Winnipeg's annual competition for Warming Huts at The Forks was designed by students at the University of Manitoba as a place for ice skaters to stop and thaw out while travelling along the frozen trails of the Red and Assiniboine Rivers. Composed of polished stainless-steel panels and one-way mirrors, the reflective rectangular box creates a mirage in its snowy surroundings. From the outside, its highly reflective skin mimics the wintery landscape around it and camouflages the cabin. Only once inside does the idea of a transparent yet enclosed structure become apparent as the one-way mirrored glass gives views up and down the trail.

Project Name	**Nuzzles**		Location	**Winnipeg, Canada**
Architect / Designer	**RAW Design**		Date	**2014**

 Nuzzles is another winning skating shelter design for Winnipeg's annual Warming Huts competition. Situated along the River Assiniboine trail, the playful folly transforms the ubiquitous summer pool noodle into a squashable cluster of wintery pom-poms. Each Nuzzle is made from hundreds of foam lengths affixed evenly over low geodesic aluminium frames, creating a secure base for the noodles and housing heating and up-lighting that diffused along the foam lengths. Assembled on-site, the brightly coloured tufts of insulating noodles provided warm, illuminated points for skaters to play in, rest on, or burrow under as they pass along the popular winter ski trail.

| Project Name **Sling Swing** | Location **Toronto, Canada** |
| Architect / Designer **WMB Studio** | Date **2015** |

Part of the annual Winter Stations project that transforms lifeguard stations on Toronto's Woodbine Beach, the Sling Swing was one of five selected designs and revises the idea of a relaxing summer deck chair into a wintery piece of public art. Following the competition theme of 'warmth', its swathes of bright orange canvas are suspended from a grid of steel poles that encompass the station and create twenty-one 'slings' in which people can swing, huddle or simply sit and contemplate the sea view. When unoccupied, the loops of fabric sway in the breeze to create a highly animated, vibrant weather vane.

| Project Name **Spontaneous City in The Tree of Heaven** | Location **London, England, UK** |
| Architect / Designer **London Fieldworks** | Date **2010** |

Clustered around two particular species of the Chinese 'Tree of Heaven' on opposite sides of London, the Spontaneous City project by London Fieldworks creates hundreds of small homes for birds and beetles. Each installation reflects the style of architecture nearby: at Duncan Terrace in Islington (pictured), the nesting and bug boxes take the form of neighbouring Georgian terraces and social housing of the 1960s. Across town, the animals' accommodation at Cremorne Gardens in the borough of Kensington and Chelsea reflects the large World's End housing estate nearby. The habitat provides more than 250 bespoke homes for birds and insects to hide, feed and nest within.

| Project Name **Animal Wall** | Location **Cardiff Bay, Wales, UK** |
| Architect / Designer **Gitta Gschwendtner** | Date **2009** |

This 50 metre (164 ft) long wall of homes for bats and birds was intended to encourage an increase in the declining natural habitat in the area and match the 1000 new human inhabitants of the apartments nearby. Commissioned by Charles Church Developments, as part of the Century Wharf development in Cardiff Bay and designed by Gitta Gschwendtner, the Animal Wall is built from custom-made woodcrete cladding. It includes four differently sized houses to accommodate 1000 new homes for small flying species of the Welsh coast. Housing a constant turnaround of winged tenants, the wall acts as a practical yet sculptural divider for animals to flit between the neighbouring residential development and riverfront.

| Project Name | **Habitable Polyhedron** | Location | **Bogota, Colombia** |
| Architect / Designer | **Manuel Villa** | Date | **2009** |

 Originally conceived as a small play area in the back garden of a suburban house, the Habitable Polyhedron is a lightweight timber pavilion that touches the earth lightly, with minimal impact on its natural surroundings. The self-supporting cabin houses a weatherproof place to play, read or relax, with built-in furniture and shelving. Its interior is filled with light from small windows and a skylight, and one fully glazed face of the polyhedron. From the outside, its cladding of hexagonal black shingles disguises the actual volume of the space and minimizes its visual impact on the surrounding gardens.

Project Name **Plankton Rolling Summer House**	Location **Wiltshire, England, UK (or elsewhere)**
Architect / Designer **Charlie Whinney Studio**	Date **2006**

Designed by Charlie Whinney Studio as a unique edition of garden furniture, this mobile work of architecture draws on his expertize in steam-bending timber to create a large-scale rolling summer house. Built from lengths of green ash and oak that were shaped and secured to form a gridshell, the double-curved structure forms a stable, lightweight sphere that spans 3 metres (9¾ ft) and can be easily rolled into different parts of a garden. The ball-like shape is inspired by plankton and its tentacular opening reveals a smaller enclosed recess inside the frame, which creates a private place to nap, read or pass time.

Commissioned by Magis for its Me Too range of children's furniture, this cardboard playhouse by Javier Mariscal is characteristic of his bold and playful style. Rendered in black and white, the small 1.6 × 1.2 × 1.3 metre (5½ × 4 × 4½ ft) home can be dismantled and flat-packed for storage. The design allows children to create their own home by colouring in and painting the white walls, as well as by adding stickers of flowers, leaves and animals that are included in the villa set. Once they've outgrown the playhouse, Villa Julia can be simply folded away or recycled, rather than languishing in a back garden as is common with conventional wooden playhouses.

| Project Name | **Zwing Bus Stop** | Location | **Krumbach, Austria** |
| Architect / Designer | **Smiljan Radić** | Date | **2014** |

in an effort to boost tourist numbers in the town, this is one of seven distinctive bus stops commissioned by a cultural association formed by the community of Krumbach, a small village in Austria's Bregenzerwald region. The Zwing Bus Stop by Chilean architect, Smiljan Radić draws on the handcraft and architectural traditions of the Bregenzerwald with an interpretation of a *Stube* or parlour. Its transparent shelter with a coffered ceiling of black concrete mimics the familiar domestic arrangement and scale of *Stuben*; though visually exposed, the small space is physically contained and houses conventional wooden chairs for waiting passengers. A small, cantilevered bird box completes the esoteric assemblage.

Project Name **Architecture for Long-Bodied-Short-Legged dog**	Date **2012**
Architect / Designer **Atelier Bow-Wow**	Location **Miami, Florida, USA (or elsewhere)**

This see-sawing timber ramp system by Atelier Bow-Wow was designed for a Dachshund Smooth and is part of the Architecture for Dogs series, commissioned by the Hara Design Institute with the Nippon Design Centre for Design Miami 2012. Each of the ramps is mounted between two open-ended wooden platforms that allows the short-legged Dachshund to pass through and walk up the slope with ease while its master reclines, allowing canine and human to connect at eye-height. The ramp system can be added to, creating a multi-level stacked atrium space for the dogs to ascend, or a parallel series of benches for dogs and owners to relax on.

Project Name **MAO'er Hutong**		Location **Beijing, China**	
Architect / Designer **Okamoto Deguchi Design (ODD)**		Date **2014**	

Contemporary urban development in Beijing has meant hundreds of *hutongs* – alleys formed by traditional courtyard houses – have been destroyed. This modest addition to a traditional northern Chinese hutong roof is an attempt to protect the ageing clay tiles and provide a shelter for cats. The V-shaped timber containers are designed to fit snugly in the groove between the curved tiled roof, at once creating a place for feline relaxation, increasing thermal insulation for the house below, and forming a catchment for weeds that tend to grow on the upper reaches of the ancient roofs and cause them to deteriorate.

Project Name **Modified Social Bench #05**	Location **New York, New York, USA**
Artist / Designer **Jeppe Hein**	Date **2015**

Part of an exhibition for the Public Art Fund at Brooklyn Bridge Park entitled *Please Touch the Art*, this is one of sixteen *Modified Social Benches* designed by Danish artist, Jeppe Hein. Reinventing the typical form of the park bench, Hein's eccentric yet functional works are a counterpoint to the rarefied art world and are designed to prompt spontaneous use by the public and to encourage social interaction. Formed in shapes that bend, rise and enclose its visitors, the benches continue Hein's earlier investigations into architecture, communication and social behaviour in urban space. Their unexpected shapes show how alterations to a ubiquitous garden object can provoke a change in use by the public.

Project Name **Famiglia Grande**	Location **Hong Kong, China (or elsewhere)**
Architect / Designer **Kacey Wong**	Date **2010**

In the wake of the 2008 financial crisis, artist Kacey Wong developed a series of stylish sleeping trolleys for wealthy people who had suddenly lost their homes. Following from Wong's earlier design of portable shelters for the homeless, Famiglia Grande is an elaborate set of folding, wheeled units for a family of four that uneasily recall a coffin in shape. Each painted steel unit contains an adjustable bed and has hinged panels that open to create a desk – an ironic mobile work-home solution that allows the declining rich to continue to look good while living on the street.

MICRO

MINI

MIÐI

MACRO

MAXI

| Project Name **Echoviren** | Location **San Francisco, California, USA** |
| Architect / Designer **Smith\|Allen Studio** | Date **2013** |

The perforated pattern of this pavilion is based on the configuration of a sequoia tree's cell, which allows the tree and this folly to have maximum strength with a minimum of volume. The pavilion was built from 585 individually printed components of plant-based polylactic acid (PLA) bio-plastic, which took two months and 10,800 hours to print, but only four days to assemble on site. Each of the 250 millimetre (9¾ in) pieces clip together to form a partially enclosed volume that stands among a redwood forest and is intended to remain in place for thirty to fifty years. In the interim, its materiality will slowly decompose and form a micro-habitat for insects, moss and birds.

| Project Name **Dispersion** | Location **Seoul, South Korea** |
| Architect / Designer **Yong Ju Lee** | Date **2015** |

Located in Seoul's Suin Line Memorial Park, Yong Ju Lee's installation *Dispersion* is a pixelated memorial to the narrow-gauge train line that operated for almost sixty years, since it opened in 1937. Formed of two disparate halves – a train carriage exterior and interior with bench seating – the appearance of the cast stainless steel sculpture solidifies or dematerializes depending on the viewer's standpoint. Each reflective body transforms from a recognizable shape into a pixellated haze; the effect is intended to provoke nostalgia and recollection of people's experience on the decommissioned train line, as well as integrating with the natural park surroundings.

Project Name	**Diogene**	Location	**Vitra Campus, Germany (or elsewhere)**
Architect / Designer	**Renzo Piano**	Date	**2014**

 In the austere spirit of the itinerant philosopher, Diogenes, this eponymous retreat is designed as a humble and self-sufficient home for contemplation, work or holidays. Measuring less than 3 metres (9¾ ft) wide, and so small enough to transport by truck, this contemporary equivalent of the ancient Roman architect Vitruvius' hut contains a sofa bed, folding table, bathroom and kitchen. The energy efficient design includes rainwater collection, solar panels and a biological toilet and is clad with insulated aluminium panels to protect inhabitants from the elements. Commissioned from Renzo Piano by Vitra the retreat is an experimental project for the public to test the pleasures and pitfalls of a minimalist house.

 These prefabricated arched homes are designed in response
to chronic shortages in stable housing that currently exists for
over 32 per cent of the world's population. Each lightweight,
affordable unit is intended to engender a stable sense of home and community and is
formed from catenary arches of solid steel. The homes are easily transported and are
enclosed by a simple corrugated metal shell, which provides both sound and thermal
insulation. Translucent plastic panels admit light to the homes that are typically off-grid.
Organized simply, each house has a small living space at ground level and a mezzanine
sleeping platform above. The Abod intention of 'one house, one family, one day' means
the components are simple enough for a small group to build a house within a day.

Project Name **Ecological Pavilion**	Location **Muttersholtz, France**
Architect / Designer **St André-Lang Architectes**	Date **2012**

 Constructed in the village of Muttersholtz for the Archi<20 competition, this 20 square metre (65¾ ft) circular pavilion is filled with corn cobs that are intended to slowly dry as the seasons pass, referencing maize dryers often seen in the neighbouring Alsatian plains. The oblique roofline responds to the position of the sun with a lower northern side and more expansive southern facade. Similarly, the light shaft in the centre of the building allows varying amounts of daylight and shade depending on the angle of the sun. Inside, a single continuous piece of furniture runs around the periphery and provides integrated storage and shelving.

This enclosed timber-lined concrete bench is part of a redevelopment by AllesWirdGut that transformed a faded steel mill in Luxembourg into a characterful urban plaza. The original, now disused, site was broad and rough, occupied by blast furnaces and other industrial equipment, so the landscape architects chose to make a more intimately scaled space with areas of seating and planting. Now interspersed with carefully considered places for the public to meet or watch events, the new interventions are built from robust materials such as concrete, wood and untreated steel and have a texture that will gain a patina over time – just like the furnaces before them.

| Project Name **PlayLAND** | Location **Paredes de Coura, Portugal** |
| Architect / Designer **LIKE Architects** | Date **2014** |

This set of three bouncy, colourful spatial interventions called playLAND were set within the public landscape of Paredes de Coura and are constructed from dozens of inflated tyre inner tubes. Created for O Mundo ao Contrário, a week-long creative event that transformed a quiet town into an artistic playground, the immersive installation takes three different states: a stage for performances, a silo-shaped tower, and a small tunnel for children to play in. Removed from the usual water-based context, each beach float serves as a modular construction element that is easily erected and allows for the creation of a light, bright structure made from functional objects, otherwise symbolic of summertime fun.

| Project Name **Open House** | Location **Melbourne, Victoria, Australia** |
| Architect / Designer **Nixon Tulloch Fortey** | Date **2011** |

Nixon Tulloch Fortey designed the Open House as part of an annual fundraising challenge for Kids Under Cover, a homeless youth charity in Australia. Restricted to a maximum footprint of 3 × 2.5 metres (9¾ × 8¼ ft) wide, the archetypal timber form immediately communicates the idea of 'home' – its gabled roof, simple front door and chimney pot replicating children's classic depictions of a house. Unfolded, the cubby house transforms into a brightly coloured and light-filled place to play – walls open to become a veranda or drawbridges, kitchen niches and cupboards provide secret hiding holes for treasures, while the operable roof hinges open to reveal a small attic space.

Project Name **Instant Untitled**	Location **Venice, Italy**
Architect / Designer **MOS Architects**	Date **2010**

 Installed in the courtyard of the American pavilion at the 2010 Venice Biennale, this inflated canopy of oversized Mylar weather balloons is tethered to the ground with green ropes to create a simple yet striking entrance to the exhibition. Designed with Andy Warhol's 1966 *Silver Clouds* installation in mind, this commission is similarly arresting, its sparkling spheres glisten in the sun, and mirror the hue and shape of neighbouring tree foliage. The floating silvery surface provides relief from the Venetian sun for visitors, who could rest and meet on the white benches arranged in the courtyard below.

| Project Name **Cat Chalet** | Location **Los Angeles, California, USA (or elsewhere)** |
| Architect / Designer **Space International** | Date **2014** |

Part of a fundraising event for Fix Nation, a charity that spays and neuters homeless cats, the Cat Chalet by Space International was imagined as a domestic retreat for feral cats. Subverting and re-scaling the familiar iconography of a gabled house, the cathouse is formed of an angular lacquered wooden 'roof', which becomes a slanted chaise longue for humans to recline on, paired by a platform beneath it for cats. The internal surface of roof and platform are lined with synthetic grass and supported by vertical columns wrapped with sisal rope. Enclosed by reflective elastic cord, which creates a protected, playful feline landscape, the Cat Chalet is also intended to evoke mid-century outdoor furniture.

Project Name	**The Cloud**	Location	**Bordeaux, France**
Architect / Designer	**Zébra3**	Date	**2010**

 Originally designed for the 2010 Panorama Biennial, The Cloud is an off-grid camping shelter that accommodates up to seven people and was sited in the Hermitage Park in Lormont, France, for one summer. Part of the Park's philosophy is to tread lightly on the earth, so the prefabricated Cloud retreat was delivered onsite, providing a place for travellers to stay without charge and equipped with neither running water nor electricity. Built from wood and plexiglass, and arranged with a pair of bunk beds inside, the white-painted folly provides the bare necessities for camping: bedding, shelter and light.

| Project Name | **Project Egg** | | Location | **Milan, Italy** |
| Architect / Designer | **Michiel van der Kley** | | Date | **2014** |

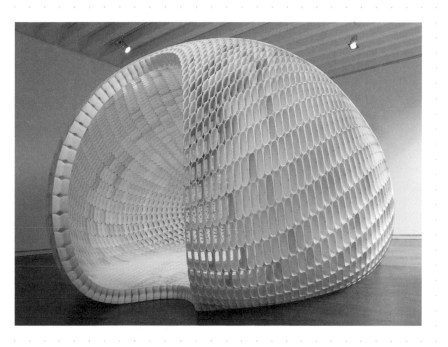

Michiel van der Kley designed this cellular, ovoid pavilion of biodegradable polylactic acid as a collaborative work, requesting contributors from around the world to 3D-print and post each of the 4,760 stones that make up its form. Spanning 5 × 4 metres (10 × 13 ft) wide, and reaching 3 metres (9¾ ft) tall, Project Egg was conceived as an organic structure in which floor, walls and ceiling merge seamlessly, comprised of an agglomeration of many small elements. As well as being unique in shape and size, the tonal variations of the individual pieces are an inherent part of the structure and reflect the crowd-sourced way in which it was produced and constructed.

Project Name **Woodland Community Garden Shed**	Location **Vancouver, Canada**	
Architect / Designer **Brendan Callander, Jason Pielak, Stella Cheung-Boyland**		Date **2014**

Crowned by a zigzagging timber roof, this prominent shed in Vancouver's Woodlands Park acts as a beacon for the community gardens and is used to host education programs as well as provide secure storage. The shed's angular beak-like roof is carefully shaped to work with the diurnal and seasonal movement of the sun, preventing shadows from falling on neighbouring garden plots. Simultaneously, its herringbone slats provide dappled shade for the internal meeting space during summer and allows light to enter in dark winter months. Enclosed by timber walls that were charred to resist decay and rot, and to prevent chemically treated wood leaching into plant beds, the blackened surfaces also act as chalkboards for lessons.

Project Name **Feral Cat Shelter**	Location **Los Angeles, California, USA (or elsewhere)**
Architect / Designer **Formation Association with Edgar Arceneaux**	Date **2014**

Designed for, and donated to, Fix Nation, an LA-based charity that spays and neuters homeless cats, the Feral Cat Shelter was created by Formation Association in collaboration with artist, Edgar Arceneaux. One of many bespoke cat shelters created for the charity benefit event, their interpretation of a cathouse is conceived as a shelter that serves both cats and people. Formed of hundreds of interleaved timber ribs held together with screws, the narrow wooden struts provide structural cross-bracing and create an undulating elongated bench. Beneath the flat upper timber surface, which is large enough to seat several people, a sheltered undercroft space is created that is perfect for shy cats to hide in, nap on or climb through.

 *This Is Not A Lovesong* is one of several commissions for follies in the grounds surrounding a 1950s villa by architect and sculptor, Andre Bloc, in Meudon, near Paris. The graphic brick installation by French artist Didier Faustino is inserted adjacent to the entrance of an existing concrete folly and derives its name from the popular 1980s anthem by English post-punk band, Public Image Limited. In contrast to the leafy green environment, the rough texture of the brick is picked out by the vibrant red paint on the walls and floor of the piece. Not only does the colour draw attention to the entry, it also acts as a frame for the space, which becomes like a small stage on which people can perform.

Part of the Kobe Biennale, Wink Space was assembled in only four hours and transformed the orthogonal interior of a shipping container into an immersive human-scale kaleidoscope for visitors to pass through and marvel at. Made from 1,100 triangular pieces of mirror peppered with fine holes, the polyhedral tunnel was zipped together and suspended from a scaffold. As people pass through the space, the colour of their clothing is reflected and scattered ten-fold, to create a disorienting visual effect of kaleidoscopic hues. By simply unzipping some seams arbitrarily, apertures are created that allow chinks of light to enter the mirrored skin, adding to the reflective visual cacophony.

| Project Name | **Township of Domestic Parts** | Location | **Venice, Italy** |
| Architect / Designer | **Jiminez Lai** | Date | **2014** |

Representing Taiwan at the 2014 Venice Biennale, the 'Township of Domestic Parts' was exhibited inside the Palazzo della Prigioni and is a descriptive collection of familiar rooms in a house that its curator, Jiminez Lai, conceived as being like small parts of a town or city.

Taking his cue from the function of rooms in modern housing, the installation included nine vibrant conceptual spaces, each designed to critique a room's particular purpose – from the centrepiece *House of Social Dining* with its circular table at the centre, to the elevated platform of the *House of Sleep*, or two-part *House of Alchemy*. Like guests in a home, visitors were invited to sit, recline or rest on the pavilions as desired.

Project Name **Drawing of a Drawing**	Location **Miami, Florida, USA**
Artist / Designer **Massimo Uberti**	Date **2014**

Creating an uninhabitable but poetic description of a home, this light installation of neon tubes by Massimo Uberti transcribes the character of a typical domestic room at real scale, including walls, door, window and furniture. The piece was commissioned by British car manufacturer Bentley as one of a series in its Bentley Elements installations for the 2014 Miami Design District. *Drawing of a Drawing* is intended to provoke reflection as viewers contemplate and move about inside the illuminated house. The neon-lit space is also a reference to Bentley's similarly lit vehicle audit bays at its manufacturing plant in Crewe, England.

Project Name **Grotto Sauna**	Location **Toronto, Canada**
Architect / Designer **Partisans**	Date **2014**

Sans Souci Island is recognized as one of the world's superior locations for viewing sunsets. With this in mind, and a prehistoric granite boulder as a site, Partisans designed a sauna that would integrate with its context and offer unobstructed views to the spectacular skies, remote inlets and forests of Georgian Bay. The small free-standing sauna is encased by a charred rectilinear timber shell; the only indication of its sinuous cedar-clad interior is an oval skylight cut into the roof. Inside, multiple sculpted sections of cedar are cut and arranged according to three-dimensional modelling and include tiered benches, a coal burner, and oval windows oriented towards the lake.

Project Name **Noa**	Location **Estonia (or anywhere)**
Architect / Designer **Jaanus Orgusaar**	Date **2011**

Noa was borne out of an invention for an economically designed living space that could be assembled from identical components and could be easily demounted. Its six-sided timber walls are shaped as identical rhombi and zigzag up and down around a level hexagonal floor plan, which creates three stable 'feet' for the wooden cabin to rest on, instead of foundations. Owing to the obtuse angles where the walls meet, the interior appears to be circular and two fish-eye windows accentuate the impact of this spherical feel. The cabin roof is formed of three more identical rhombi, which, like the walls, are made from iron oxide-soaked wood. Because of its modular format, the house can be readily extended.

| Project Name **Cityscope** | Location **Cologne, Germany (or elsewhere)** |
| Architect / Designer **Marco Hemmerling** | Date **2008** |

Part of the architectural festival Plan08, this faceted iridescent pavilion by Marco Hemmerling was installed in the forecourt of Cologne Central Station and is formed of triangular units mounted on an aluminium frame. The angular panes of Cityscope create a kaleidoscopic view of the surrounding urban environment that Hemmerling intended as a tool that challenges our usual way of seeing the city. Instead of an orderly arrangement of a built environment, the triangulated envelope highlighted and dislocated elements, such as the cropped Gothic spires of Cologne Cathedral nearby. At night, the translucent panels glowed in accord with the cityscape around it, at once revealing the interior contents and creating a luminous colourful folly.

 The Winter Stations competition was established to enliven the utilitarian lifeguard stations along the edge of Lake Ontario during frosty months. Snowcone is one of five projects chosen for the inaugural event. Designed by architectural students Lily Jeon and Diana Koncan from the Ryerson University Department of Architectural Science, the small folly was fabricated from steel conduits, nylon zip ties and coloured acrylic. Fabricated with a team of university colleagues and assembled from prefabricated components in just six hours, the project is a hybrid between the structural properties of a pinecone and the insulating properties of an igloo. In warm weather Snowcone filters a colourful kaleidoscope of light; during snowy conditions its insulating shell protects visitors from the cold.

Project Name **Chameleon Cabin**	Location **Sweden (or elsewhere)**	Date **2014**

Architect / Designer **White Arkitekter with Happy and Göteborgstryckeriet**

This lightweight, moveable hut is formed of ninety-five modules of corrugated paper, which can be unfolded, erected and extended anywhere without requiring planning permission. Striking to look at, its name derives from the appearance of the cabin that changes depending on your viewpoint, segueing from a matte marbled black, to black-and-white stripes, to a white faux marble finish. The faux stone finishes are intended to elevate the modest material of the paper cabin, which weighs only 100 kilograms (220 lbs) and is self-supporting, based on a hanger construction method. Punctuated by yolk-yellow coloured windows, the proportions of the cabin recall a traditional Swedish *friggebod* or small shed.

Part architecture, part sculpture, this temporary piece, *Dwelling* by Dutch artist Krijn de Koning, was installed on the south terrace of the Turner Contemporary and is formed of a series of walls set at an angle and cut open to form differently sized windows and doorways for visitors to navigate under, through and over. The perpendicular planes of the maze are each painted in bright colours, referencing traditional colourful British beach huts, and abut the glazed facade and robust concrete balustrades. Open to the sky, the vibrant labyrinth confuses the eye further as patterns of shadows shift across its surfaces throughout the day.

Project Name **Shell.ter Pavilion**	Location **Vila Nova de Cerveira, Portugal**
Architect / Designer **LIKE Architects**	Date **2012**

From afar, the workings of this intricate white tunnel seem obscure, but closer inspection reveals its fabrication made solely from everyday plastic deck chairs. The diverting summer installation in the Portuguese Parque de Lazer do Castelinho by LIKE Architects stands almost 3 metres (9¾ ft) tall and stretches 6 metres (19¾ ft) in length, and was designed to provide shade and seating for the public during the Cerveira Creative Camp. Though its materials are of humble origin, the stacked, incised form creates complex shadows and patterns as the sun passes overhead. At the close of the season, the structure was simply disassembled, minimising its environmental impact.

Project Name **Solar Bytes Pavilion**	Location **Ohio, USA**	
Architect / Designer **Design.Lab.Workshop/Brian Peters**	Date **2014**	

Constructed from ninety-four individual modules – or 'bytes' – this arched pavilion illustrates the potential of increasingly sophisticated technologies used in the making and performance of buildings. Initiated by Brian Peters as part of the Design.Lab.Workshop interdisciplinary studio at Kent State College, the self-supporting pavilion is composed of digitally printed translucent plastic blocks, embedded with integrated solar-powered LEDs. Each block fits together to form an arch that spans from east to west, orientated to maximize daily solar gain. At night, the solar energy collected by the cells over the course of a day creates a light-emitting display that varies depending on the amount of cloud cover, rain or intensity of sunlight.

| Project Name **Artists Retreat** | Location **Fiskars, Finland** |
| Architect / Designer **O-to-1** | Date **2011** |

 Designed as a live-work studio for the artist owner and other artistic guests, the unusual geometry of this one-bedroom house derives from a quarter of an octagon. Decreasing in width from the back to the front, the sloping walls converge, enclosing a sleeping loft and amenities to the rear and a studio workspace in the centre, which opens via a full-width hinged door to a triangular deck that tapers to the narrow end of the wedge. Clad in locally-sourced wood that is painted in a yellow hue to match historic Finnish homes nearby, the studio is protected from heavy snowfall by its titanium roof.

Project Name **Le Plongeoir**	Location **Muttersholtz, France**
Architect / Designer **Spray Architecture**	Date **2012**

Located in a wooded area of Muttersholtz in the east of France, this simple timber and polycarbonate pavilion was designed by Spray Architecture. Appropriately enough, the studio designed this project of 'graffitecture' – architecture that gains expression as its shell is increasingly sprayed with graffiti. Held lightly aloft from the ground by timber stilts, the 14 square metre (46 sq ft) pavilion is a place for rest, play and self-expression. Its exterior and interior slowly transformed over time, as more graffiti artists added their mark. Arranged in an oblique polygon that rises from a low entrance, up seat-wide stairs, to a higher lookout point, Le Plongeoir's exterior also follows this low-high arrangement, with more dense painting closer to the ground, and less spray near the top.

| Project Name **Rucksack House** | Location **Germany (or elsewhere)** |
| Architect / Designer **Stefan Eberstadt** | Date **2004** |

 Suspended from the roofs of apartment blocks in various locations around Germany, the Rucksack House is a habitable, moveable 9 square metre (29½ sq ft) addition for small spaces, based on the archetypical hideaway of a tree house. Designed by Stefan Eberstadt, the house is held aloft by steel cables that are anchored to the existing building, and provides a platform for reading or sleeping high above the street below. The welded steel cage is clad with plywood externally and lined with a birch veneer, punctuated by acrylic insertions, which create the ultimate place to spy from. Inside, sections of the walls fold down to reveal a desk, shelves and reading platform, all of which are held in place by magnetic fastenings in the wall recesses.

| Project Name **Pig House** | Location **Ramsen, Germany** |
| Architect / Designer **Naumann Architektur** | Date **2003** |

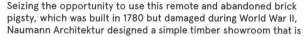 Seizing the opportunity to use this remote and abandoned brick pigsty, which was built in 1780 but damaged during World War II, Naumann Architektur designed a simple timber showroom that is inserted within the original walls of the sty. Manufactured offsite and craned into position, the new room is made from a four-sided frame and floor of sealed Finnish plywood that is incised with openings for windows and doors, mimicking the original animal house. Raised above the ground on a concrete plinth and with silicone-sealed glazing, both old and new walls are protected from the elements by a zinc titanium-finished roof, which extends beyond the brick perimeter.

Project Name **Unterkrumbach Nord Bus Stop**	Location **Krumbach, Austria**
Architect / Designer **Ensamble Studio**	Date **2014**

One of seven bus stops designed by internationally-recognized architects for the small Austrian village of Krumbach, the Unterkrumbach Nord shelter by Ensamble Studio is a stacked arrangement of rough, untreated oak planks that emulate the way timber is laid to dry in workshops of this region, the Bregenzerwald. Each layer of wood is organized perpendicular to the one below it, creating open and enclosed slices that are sculpted to include an overhanging roof and benches for passengers. Part of the commission was to work with local expertize and craftspeople and the raw untreated finish of this shelter is intentional, giving an olfactory and spatial experience that is regionally specific.

Marking the entrance to Central Park and built in celebration of the State of New York's Marriage Equality Act of 2011, this pop-up cardboard chapel was designed by Z-A Studio as a temporary venue for twelve couples to marry on 30 July of that year. Formed of 130 wedges of recycled honeycomb cardboard joined together with wood glue and affixed to the plywood, the Studio imagined Kiss as an allegory for marriage: two separate halves made of the same DNA joining as one. Designed in just three days and assembled in only two hours, the two unique wall sections create a stable structure that enfolds the celebrant and the couple.

Project Name **Self-Sufficient Modules**	Location **Matosinhos, Portugal (or elsewhere)**
Architect / Designer **Cannatà & Fernandes**	Date **2003**

 Designed as a simple modular and easily transported structure, the Self-Sufficient Modules by Cannatà & Fernandes were first produced for the Concreta Exhibition in 2003. Though shown here as a small housing solution, the modules can equally be used as a bar, kiosk, environmental observatory or for fire surveillance. The flexibility of use is due to its modular design that allows it to be installed in places with little infrastructural access, such as parks, beaches or forested areas. Only 27 square metres (88½ sq ft) in total, the interior spaces are efficiently designed with all amenities neatly tucked into the 9 metre (29½ ft) long walls, which are framed at each end by a full-height window.

Project Name **Glamping**	Location **Yang-Pyeong, South Korea**
Architect / Designer **ArchiWorkshop**	Date **2013**

 Embracing the popularity of glamorous camping, or 'glamping', ArchiWorkshop devised a lightweight system for small-scale Glamping units installed in a remote site in Yang-Pyeong. The two versions – a pebble-like Stacking Doughnut (pictured) and the longer extendable tubular Modular Floor version – both sit on steel footings. Formed from prefabricated tubular steel frames that can be simply bolted together, the units have a double-skinned membrane of fluoropolymer material that allows the structures to breathe but also protects against rain and snow. The Glamping units are designed for maximum comfort and include a protected veranda, bespoke sofa beds and an indoor bathroom that is disguised behind large-scale wall paintings.

Project Name **Forest Retreat**	Location **Doksy, Czech Republic**
Architect / Designer **Uhlik Architekti**	Date **2014**

Hidden amid an elysian landscape of woods, meadows and boulders, this retreat for a city-dwelling client to rest, meditate or socialise occupies only 16 square metres (52½ sq ft) and is partially balanced atop a large rock. Two large glazed openings provide entry and views out of the lozenge-shaped form: guests enter at the lower level onto a flat platform, with four broad stairs rising to an upper platform and picture window from which to contemplate tree canopies. Designed and built by the architects in collaboration with a nearby carpenter and blacksmith, the retreat is a local affair – its boards and joists were harvested from fallen trees on the property. Blackened walls provide protection and camouflage while the asphalt roof ensures the cabin is waterproof.

Project Name **Ta di Ôtô**	Location **Hanoi, Vietnam (or elsewhere)**
Architect / Designer **Bureau A**	Date **2013**

 Among the throngs of bicycles and scooters in Hanoi, this seven-storey tower on a tricycle creates a distinctive mobile street stall and is a performance space for a multitude of uses. Designed for local Hanoi bar and cultural centre, Ta di Ôtô, the 4 metre (13 ft) high open framework of blue-painted steel was manufactured and adapted to fit the tricycle on the outskirts of the city, then simply cycled in. Like many of Hanoi's itinerant and multi-purpose trading stalls, Ta di Ôtô's bike can go anywhere and be adopted for a variety of uses by simply adding or subtracting elements such as plastic stools, cooking equipment or stage sets.

| Project Name **D-Tunnel** | Location **Miami, Florida, USA (or elsewhere)** |
| Architect / Designer **Kenya Hara** | Date **2012** |

The D-Tunnel was designed by Kenya Hara and is one of thirteen works of dog architecture – a playful initiative led by the Hara Design Institute and Nippon Design Centre that commissioned leading architects and designers to create dog-sized architecture. Cut from two sheets of plywood, the D-Tunnel's twelve panels and three timber struts are simply screwed together and act as a 'scale modifier' – an architectural apparatus that is intended to redress the imbalance in size between humans and animals. In this case, the tunnel is specifically designed for a tiny tea cup poodle and allows the dog to ascend four small steps sheltered within it to meet its human at eye-level.

| Project Name **Wood Box** | Location **Montpellier, France** |
| Architect / Designer **Atelier Vecteur** | Date **2012** |

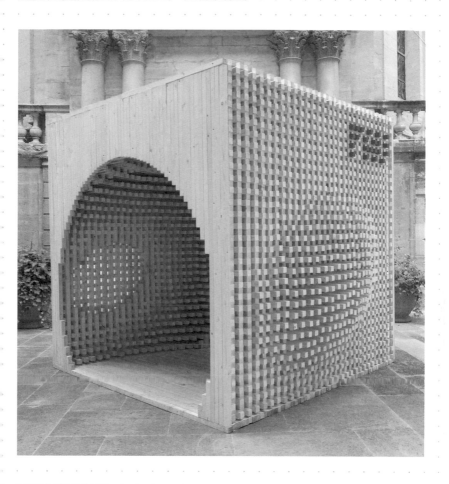

Part of the annual Festival of Lively Architecture held in Montpellier, Wood Box appears to be a deceptively simple timber cube stationed in the centre of the Place Saint-Côme courtyard, one of twelve sites that host the event. Depending on a guest's viewpoint, the temporary installation morphed from a rectilinear structure composed of thousands of slats, to an ovoid form that seems to bulge beyond its orthogonal boundaries. Created by an interlocking grid of square profiled laths, the folly's interior was pared away to form a habitable sphere-shaped space. Outside, the protruding laths hint at the lively internal volume, attracting visitors to discover information about the festival.

Project Name **OTIS**	Location **Vermont, USA (or elsewhere)**
Architect / Designer **Lucas Brown/Green Mountain College**	Date **2013**

Designed to be towed on a standard trailer by a four-cylinder car, this small transportable house is a recent exploration into small-scale living built by students of Green Mountain College under the direction of Environmental Studies Professor, Lucas Brown. The curvaceous timber home provides 21 square metres (68¾ sq ft) of living area and is powered by a single 120-watt solar panel. Nicknamed OTIS (Optimal Travelling Independent Space), the tiny self-sufficient house also includes a rainwater system to supply the kitchen and bathroom. OTIS suggests a more modest and ecologically minded alternative to the grander and more permanent dwellings that typify the American Dream.

Project Name	**Kolonihavehus**	Location	**Copenhagen, Denmark (or elsewhere)**
Artist / Designer	**Tom Fruin Studio**	Date	**2010**

 Standing in the Royal Danish Library Plaza, *Kolonihavehus* is a luminous reinterpretation of traditional Danish garden sheds, which were once intended to provide modest refuges for state workers living in crowded urban environments. A simple steel frame delineates the 3.5 square metre (11½ sq ft) gabled hut and holds hundreds of pieces of acrylic sheet, which emulates the effect of stained glass and casts vibrant patterns within and beyond the shed walls. Each of the colourful fragments was retrieved and scavenged from local sources in Copenhagen, including an obsolete Perspex distributor and rubbish bins outside the Danish Architecture Centre – continuing Fruin's interest in reinterpreting found materials.

| Project Name **Refugi Lieptgas** | Location **Flims, Switzerland** |
| Architect / Designer **Nickisch Sano Walder Architects** | Date **2012** |

This tiny Alpine refuge in Flims is marked by its concave ribbed concrete shell, which was cast from aging convex timber logs that once clad the chalet. Housing a modern two-storey cabin for eating, sleeping and bathing, the local authorities required the new building to be replaced with something that had 'the character of the preceding cabin'. Though this refuge has the same footprint and form as its predecessor, it inverts the log shape of the facade. The upper level houses living and dining rooms while bathroom and bedroom are downstairs in the renovated cellar. Both rooms have just a single large window that frames views of the surrounding landscape.

| Project Name **Paul's Shed for The Wish List** | Location **London, England, UK** |
| Architect / Designer **Paul Smith with Nathalie de Leval** | Date **2014** |

Part of the 2014 London Design Festival at the Victoria & Albert Museum, this garden shed was designed in response to fashion designer Paul Smith's wish for the perfect addition to his home. Working with furniture designer, Nathalie de Leval, the 3 × 3 metre (9¾ × 9¾ ft) shed is set on a revolving platform in order to optimize sunshine and is imagined as an essential 'room with a view'. Its simple gabled structure is built from horizontal weatherboards of thermally modified American ash, a process that renders the normally pale-coloured wood a dark chocolate brown. The simple shed is filled with objects of significance to Smith, which are revealed in a single full-height glazed wall.

 Situated in the courtyard facing the fifteenth-century Basilica of Santa Maria Novella in Florence, these Rolling Houses were designed by Avatar Architettura for the city's White Night celebrations curated by Valentina Gensini. Constructed from timber lengths to create an approximately circular form, each house is pierced by an irregular internal shape, which creates a platform on which to rest, eat, read or chat. Distinguished by these mutable interior spaces and brightly coloured walls, the house can be rolled into different positions – instantly changing the interior characteristics and the likely use of these minimum parcels of urban space.

| Project Name **Skating Shelters** | Location **Winnipeg, Canada** |
| Architect / Designer **Patkau Architects** | Date **2011** |

Huddled against the freezing winter winds of Winnipeg's prairies, these six folded plywood shelters provide respite for ice skaters traversing the city's popular and lengthy Red and Assiniboine River trails. Each of the three pairs of shelters is made from two layers of flexible plywood that wraps around a triangular base and forms a wedge-shaped spine and ridge members, mitigating the weight of snow. Small incisions in the plywood accommodate the bending stress of timber and create narrow light wells. Like small booths, the interiors have plywood stools and fit only a few people at once. Though the position of the shelters on the frozen river appears randomly assigned, they are carefully orientated to create an open yet protected space for people to converse and mingle in.

 Lifted 11 metres (36 ft) above ground, and encircling a mature oak tree, this is an adult-sized tree house by Andreas Werning of Baumraum, who has made an art of designing bespoke tree houses and suspended tents. The house is supported by two steel poles embedded into the tree trunk, and is accessed by a spiral steel staircase from the client's garage roof. Guests enter via a trapdoor in the deck to reach the small elliptical space that houses a double bed tucked into one end, and an upholstered window seat with built-in storage.

Set atop a Chilean hillside that was previously logging territory, this storage facility and shelter provides a resting place for hunters in the winter and for hikers in summer. The partially open, rectilinear wooden deck overlooks the Villarrica Volcano from one end and the Calafquén and Panguipulli Lakes from the other, and was built from leftover logs recovered from the site. The project led by Rodrigo Sheward Giordano with University of Talca architecture students, was an exercise in understanding and building architecture. The group sawed and prepared the wood on site, then constructed the project from 96 pieces of 0.25 × 3 metre (¾ × 9¾ ft) timber lengths. The resulting platform includes an integrated timber ladder, which optimizes views from the roof.

Project Name **Eco Pavilion**	Location **Mexico City, Mexico**
Architect / Designer **MMX**	Date **2011**

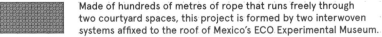 Made of hundreds of metres of rope that runs freely through two courtyard spaces, this project is formed by two interwoven systems affixed to the roof of Mexico's ECO Experimental Museum. Crisscrossing high above visitors, the ropes form screens that act as three-dimensional surfaces of varying densities. Creating confined areas for visitors to pass through, the screens reconfigure the previously open courtyard and create different perspectives that shift depending on how visitors traverse the space. Diurnal changes in light and shadow add to the complexity of the effect so that the experience inside the pavilion fluctuates according to the time of day.

The Bird's Nest, designed by Swedish architects Inrednin Gsgruppen is one of several bespoke hotel rooms commissioned by the Tree Hotel group. Similar to other accommodation on the remote forest site, the design has an ecological bent and aims to impact minimally on the natural environment. Supported by the surrounding trees and reached by a retractable ladder, The Birds Nest is held aloft and encased by a web of branches that mimic a real bird's nest albeit at human scale. The wooden theme continues inside, with timber panels cladding the bedrooms, small kitchen and bathroom. Small round windows are punched through the walls at strategic points and partially covered by the twigs, giving visitors privacy as well as allowing views out.

Project Name **Garagenatelier**	Location **Herdern, Switzerland**
Architect / Designer **Peter Kunz Architektur**	Date **1999**

 Juxtaposing the manmade forms of architecture and automobiles with the natural gradient and grasses of a meadow, this project houses a private car collection in the municipality of Herdern. Embedded into a sloping hillside, the subterranean garage can hold up to eight cars and is revealed by five glass-fronted cubes, each large enough to display one car. Marked by partially buried orthogonal cast concrete shells, the garage is accessed from a driveway that passes through one of the cubes and leads into the concrete bunker-like space. The interior is lit by sunlight from the large glazed apertures and ranks of stark fluorescent light tubes.

Project Name **Back Side Flip 360°**	Location **Montpellier, France**
Architect / Designer **Ateliers O-S Architectes**	Date **2008**

 Installed temporarily in the courtyard of the Hotel Saint-Côme in Montpellier as part of the Festival des Architectures Vives 2008, this tunnel of cardboard packaging boxes is lined with gold foil, creating a modest yet kaleidoscopic intervention in the historic environment. From afar, the matte finish of the stacked 400 × 400 millimetre (15¾ × 15¾ ft) boxes is not distinctive, but as festival-goers approach the project, its striking reflective qualities inside are revealed. Visitors can pass through the staggered form of the golden interior, which fractures reflections – or can simply pass by the structure that also acts as a contrasting frame to the stone courtyard and colonnades.

Project Name **Vulkan Beehive**	Location **Oslo, Norway**
Architect / Designer **Snøhetta**	Date **2014**

 Concerned by the widely reported decline of bees around the world, Norwegian architecture studio Snøhetta responded with this pair of honey-coloured hives. Sitting atop the Mathallan food and dance centre in Oslo, the hives raise public awareness while also creating a bespoke honey product for the store. Designed in collaboration with beekeeper Heier Du Rietz, the timber structures are each formed of two intersecting hexagonal volumes and house 160,000 bees in total. Bees access the hives via a low, narrow landing lip and slit and both volumes are intended to mimic not only the spatially efficient shape of a honeycomb, but also its decorative pattern, which is used as an embossed motif on the golden timber facades.

| Project Name **Kreod Pavilion** | Location **London, England, UK** |
| Architect / Designer **Chun Qing Li/KREOD** | Date **2012** |

 Resembling over-scaled seed heads, these three cocoon-like pods housed the official venues for gymnastics and basketball finals and wheelchair basketball at the London 2012 Olympics Games. Each 20 square metre (65½ sq ft) pavilion stands 3.2 metres (10½ ft) high and is formed of a series of modular interlocking hexagonal forms that are assembled to create complex, secure and weatherproof structures. Internally, the skins are clad with tensile fabric and encased by a structural exterior made of Kebony – a sustainable alternative to tropical hardwoods or woods treated with preservatives. The pods can be used singly as stand-alone enclosures, or combined to form a variety of larger spatial configurations.

Project Name **Cat House**	Location **Los Angeles, California, USA (or elsewhere)**
Architect / Designer **HOK**	Date **2014**

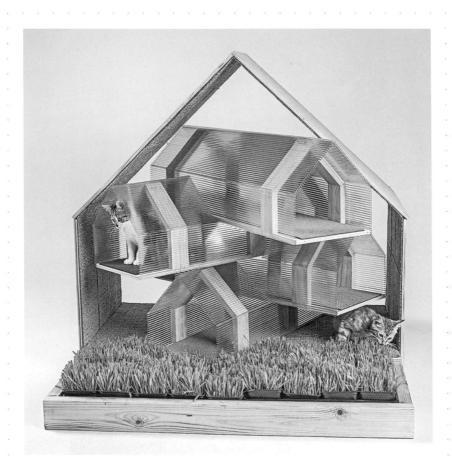

 This stack of translucent housing for cats was designed by HOK as part of a fundraising event organized by Architects for Animals for the cat charity, FixNation. Reworking the familiar domestic motif of a gabled roof, the house for cats has four smaller house-shaped units fitted together within a larger timber gable and framed by a miniature front lawn. The multi-level shelter makes a playful assemblage of functions for cats that are often discrete, providing places to hide, jump, climb, scratch or sleep. Constructed from only three materials found off-the-shelf – acrylic sheet, timber panels, and artificial grass – the project is ripe for replication by DIY enthusiasts.

Project Name **Pavillions Wonderryck Natura Docet**	Location **Wonderryck, The Netherlands**
Architect / Designer **Studio Makkink and Bey**	Date **2013**

One of three timber pavilions installed in the diverse landscape garden at Wonderryck, this house-shaped 'indoor biotope' by Makkink and Bey diverges from the idea of a traditional wooden park bench for humans and instead serves as a verdant resting point for animals. Humans can watch the animation within the prairie house but are barred from entering by wooden beams. A mix of grasses, shrubs and a fruit tree are planted inside to encourage inhabitation and nesting throughout the year. Providing homes for birds, insects and small animals, the flora helps to protect the local fauna while the distinctive wooden pavilion piques interest in visitors and draws attention to the natural order within the grounds.

Project Name **Umbrella Sky**	Location **Águeda, Portugal**
Architect / Designer **Sextafeira, Produções**	Date **2014**

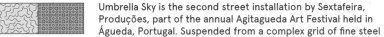 Umbrella Sky is the second street installation by Sextafeira, Produções, part of the annual Agitagueda Art Festival held in Águeda, Portugal. Suspended from a complex grid of fine steel wires, the bright umbrellas hang above the central city streets, forming a canopy that covers almost 3000 square metres (9842½ sq ft). In vibrant hues of pink, blue, yellow, purple and green the umbrellas were selected to contrast with the typically dull greys of the urban environment, creating a celebratory spatial experience for festival-goers. More than 3000 umbrellas were used, spread over different locations, and were installed by a small team in just one week.

 Wrapped with hundreds of metres of blue ribbed plastic tubing, the Blue Tube Bar is a vibrant, hirsute watering hole temporarily installed for the Portuguese festival, Queima das Fitas do Porto. The bar is constructed from a rectilinear wooden frame, inserted with a hinged, perforated timber hatch that slides opens to reveal the bar. The simple timber framework is disguised by coils of blue tubing held in place with standard nylon cable ties, which gives the bar a 'hairy' finish. Because of the simple construction methods and standard building materials, almost all the elements could be disassembled and re-used once the festival closed.

This studio and gallery near Hanging Rock, Victoria is an unusual interpretation of a typical Aussie country shed and is designed to display the artwork of the client's late wife. Its distinctive arrowhead form is the result of a brief for an inexpensive gallery space that could withstand the harsh Australian climate and also maximize security. Lined with plywood and clad with lapped galvanized steel sheets, the robust shed has two V-shaped angular facades that are fixed with timber screens: by day these filter light into the building without compromising security; by night the chevron-patterned lattice casts variegated light onto the BBQ area.

Part of playground facilities designed by Haugen Zohar Arkitekter, this Fireplace for Children in the Norwegian town of Trondheim required ingenuity: transforming a limited budget into an engaging focal point. Housing a fire pit set into a concrete plinth, the playful outdoor space rises up into a hollow teardrop shape and is formed from short lengths of discarded timber, reclaimed from a local building site. Standing eighty layers tall, each wooden band is composed of twenty-eight pieces of pine that vary in size and position to create the striated chimney-like form. Small pieces of oak separate each layer, allowing light and air to pass through the porous facade. When required, the fireplace can be secured from children by sliding across a curved door that echoes the double-curvature of the folly.

Project Name Spirit Shelter	Location Germany (or elsewhere)
Architect / Designer Allergutendinge	Date 2010

 While studying at the Bauhaus University in Weimar, Matthias Prüger, Manuel Rauwolf and Ulrike Wetzel designed and built this small retreat, which was imagined as a meditative place for study, contemplation and self-discovery. Assembled from sheets of fibreglass-reinforced plastic panels, and with an interior simply clad in unfinished timber, the Spirit Shelter is designed to be easily demounted and reassembled in rural locations, offering inhabitants a secluded environment for introspection. The components of this tiny space metamorphose: the front wall folds down to become a deck, the roof opens to the sky and numerous storage niches are built-in – including the table and ladder treads.

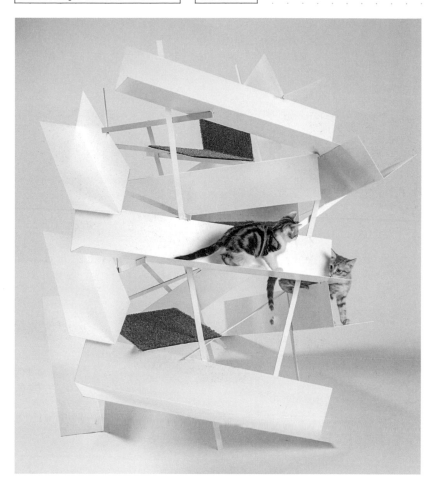

ConCATenate is the multi-storey response by Lehrer Architects to design a cathouse for Architecture for Animals. Made for a one-off charity fundraising event for FixNation, the ConCATenate design draws on the etymology of its name: a linear processional series of elements that cats can use to ascend the 1.3 metre (4¼ ft) tall structure. Made of sixteen-gauge sheet metal, cats can climb the right-angled shelving to reach any one of three platforms, each lined with brilliantly blue-coloured artificial grass. The cacophony of angled white planes and struts creates a kind of feline jungle gym that frames the open-air shelter and provides shade from the Californian sun.

| Project Name **Tape City** | Location **Melbourne, Victoria, Australia** |
| Architect / Designer **Numen/For Use** | Date **2011** |

 The first project by Numen/For Use outside of Europe, Tape City at Federation Square in Melbourne was commissioned as part of the city's Creative Programme, which focused on the social impact of large-scale public art. Made of 30 kilometres (18 mi) of packing tape, this edition of Tape City stretched the full 16 metre (52½ ft) length of the venue's Western Terrace, spanning like an over-scaled web across the plaza. Its form was dictated by the context, projecting 6 metres (19¾ ft) above ground from the external walls of the SBS building. Visitors to the project could explore the semi-translucent interior of the tunnels, which filter light through the carapace and conjure the effect of a chrysalis.

Project Name **Mirage Pavilion**	Location **Hajógyári, Budapest**
Architect / Designer **Studio Nomad**	Date **2014**

This 'almost invisible' installation by Studio Nomad was commissioned for the summer music festival, Sziget, in Budapest on a forested island in the middle of the Danube River. In contrast to the increasingly high-tech entertainment in European clubs, Studio Nomad made an event pavilion using simple materials and construction methods. Drawing on the idea of geometric patterns used on 'dazzle ships' in World War I, the pavilion is composed of 1,200 mirrored plastic squares arranged in a chequerboard pattern and suspended from trees by transparent cord. Forming a 23 metre (75½ ft) long wall, the pattern is created by alternating mirrored surfaces and open squares, which simultaneously give views through, and of, the surrounding forest to disorientating visual effect.

| Project Name **The Truffle** | Location **Costa de Morte, Spain** |
| Architect / Designer **Ensamble Studio** | Date **2010** |

 This simple holiday home in northern Spain overlooks the Atlantic Ocean and followed an unusual construction process involving concrete, hay bales, a cow, and a very large hole. Described as 'a piece of nature built with earth, full of air', the retreat was made by pouring concrete into a deep pit, filled with 50 cubic metres (164 cu ft) of stacked hay bales, which formed the internal cavity. Once set, the concrete was revealed by clawing away soil to reveal a cabin with an earthen texture and colour. A calf grazed on the bales inside and, one year later, the undulating interior moulded by the hay was revealed. Several simple incisions into the concrete 'truffle' allowed for insertion of the entry and picture window, completing this lithic seaside retreat.

This gleaming chicken coop is the result of a commission for Architecture Research Office (ARO) to design a home for hens in the back yard of an East Hamptons house. Reminiscent of a miniature airstream trailer, the 18 square metre (59 sq ft) coop is clad with hundreds of bent aluminium shingles that contrast with the rustic timber framed structure within. Having analyzed the optimum conditions for a coop according to hen size, safety and ease of egg collection, ARO created a simple vaulted tunnel with roosting rails along one wall and nesting boxes opposite them. A hinged door in the aluminium cladding gives access to the eggs but hens are protected from foxes and other predators by a large front door. Lighting and radiant heating give the final touches to this eloquent avian address.

 Entitled Mount Pug, this constellation of timber struts incised with carefully matching notches forms Japanese architect Kengo Kuma's design of a wooden shelter for a pug – part of the Hara Design Institute and Nippon Design Centre's initiative of Architecture for Dogs. Assembled without nails or glue, the seventy-four branches of 600 millimetre (23½ in) deep plywood interlock to form hexagonal and triangular shapes that are self-supporting and rise to a gentle mound standing 800 millimetres (31½ ft) high. This shallow dome creates a semi-sheltered environment for pugs to play or sleep under and the precise notching system also allows canine toys or snacks to be suspended from the timber mesh.

Project Name **Bloomberg Pavilion**	Location **Tokyo, Japan**	
Architect / Designer **Akihisa Hirata Architecture Office**	Date **2011**	

 Commissioned by the Tokyo Museum of Art in a collaborative initiative with Bloomberg, this pavilion by Akihisa Hirata's practice houses solo exhibitions by young Tokyo artists and performers. The walls of its simple triangular footprint grow in a series of isosceles triangles that unfold from the roof plane and form an expanded crisp white surface. Known as a 'hyplane' – a new type of polyhedra formed of tiled hyperbolic triangles – the billowing form was derived from the structure of a tree and creates an arresting symbol that draws attention to the Museum's new cultural and artistic remit.

| Project Name **Outlandia** | Location **Glen Nevis, Scotland, UK** | Date **2010** |

Architect / Designer **London Fieldworks with Malcolm Fraser Architects**

 Nestled in a copse of spruce and larch near the foot of Ben Nevis, this artists' studio and field station is designed in the vein of a simple shelter of a bothy or Japanese poetry pavilion, offering a peaceful place to reflect and create. The simple room sits atop a single pillar embedded into a steep slope and looks akin to the tree trunks that surround it. Clad with timber – some of which was harvested to clear the site – the structure is accessed from a wooden path that leads across a bridge to the entry. Inside, a large picture window is oriented towards the glen and opens to a small balcony; above the main studio is a mezzanine platform for sleeping or resting.

| Project Name **Re-Creation** | Location **Venice, Italy** | Date **2014** |

Architect / Designer **Anssi Lassila, OOPEAA Office for Peripheral Architecture**

Expressing the variation and specificity of local materials and techniques, this Finnish hut was one of a pair commissioned by Juulia Kauste at the Museum of Finnish Architecture for 'Re-Creation' at the 2014 Venice Biennale. The primitive hut is designed using traditional Finnish materials and building techniques, and assembled by a Finnish carpenter. Formed of four tapering walls of horizontally-stacked spruce laths cut into chunky dimensions, the hut rises up and interlocks at the corners with a variation of a traditional lap joint. A simple oblong entry leads inside, where the inclined walls frame a rectilinear skylight. The hut's fraternal twin was a circular version constructed of vertically stacked bamboo and realized by a Chinese team, with Shenzhen Bi-City Biennale of Urbanism/Architecture.

MICRO

MINI

MIDI

MACRO

MAXI

 Inspired by the energy-efficient geodesic domes of Richard Buckminster Fuller, the Bucky Bar was a short-lived street installation and bar in Rotterdam, made entirely of interconnected red umbrellas clustered around a lamppost. The octagonal shape of the umbrellas happily approximates the geodesic rules devised by Fuller, enabling this common object to transform into a modular tensile skin that spanned above several hundred revellers and rested on two self-supporting points. Though local police closed down the bar the same evening it was mounted, the temporary shelter conveyed the architects' interest in the power of spontaneous and practical architectural solutions for urban settings.

| Project Name | Ring Dome | | Location | New York, New York, US |
| Architect / Designer | Minsuk Cho | | Date | 2008 |

Fifteen hundred children's hula-hoops form the main modular component of this filigree dome, commissioned from Minsuk Cho by the Storefront for Art and Architecture to celebrate its twenty-fifth anniversary. Held together with 12,000 cable ties, the multitude of intersecting hoops sit above a larger network of overlapping metal rings, which creates the basic dome shape. The white hooped pavilion appeared as an ethereal cover by day and was lit at night to give a diffuse glow to the park surroundings, drawing attention to the concerts, discussions, and events held within it.

Project Name	Temporary Playground	Location	Wolfsburg, Germany (or elsewhere)
Architect / Designer	Topotek 1	Date	2004

These twenty-four inflatable pink objects accompanied by fifteen foam cubes were created for Wolfsburg's State Garden Show by German landscape architects, Topotek 1. The oversized, soft forms were strewn about the lawn like taut skins, their pink hues and indeterminate use attracting the attention of young and old who lolled on, climbed through, rolled with or simply gazed at the unusual bulging objects. In contrast to the natural surroundings of the Allerpark, the pink temporary playground offered a collection of over-scaled toys that are also flexible sculptures – their candyfloss hues can be spilled onto, and scattered across, any public space, transforming it into a light-hearted place to play.

 Designed by Phillip Schöne and Emma Penttinen for Essex County Council, this 45 square metre (147½ sq ft) nylon folly was a response to a commission for an interactive arts project for The People Speak collective, with assistance from Inflate. Its swollen pale body creates a distinctive and recognizable pavilion for the housing estate in which it stands, giving local residents an entertaining, mobile and easily-assembled place for many different users to meet. Punctuated by three different openings and animated by colourful Perspex windows, Inflatable Space encourages movement through the pavilion. Developed through a process of public consultation, its bulbous body evokes the visual language of insects – bugs and butterflies being especially popular with local children.

Project Name **Inflato Dumpster**	Location **New York, New York, USA**
Architect / Designer **John Locke/Joaquin Reyes**	Date **2014**

 Funded in part by a successful Kickstarter campaign, this inflatable classroom installed within a dumpster is in the heart of Manhattan Island and gives 15 square metres (49¼ sq ft) of weatherproof space for use by the public. The bubble is enclosed by an inflated membrane of translucent polyethylene sandwiched with a layer of Mylar, which creates an insulating protective barrier. When aerated, the Inflato Dumpster provides room for free workshops, documentary screenings and musical performances. Its almost weightless silvery membrane contrasts with the heavy, rectilinear steel skip in which the civic-minded project sits, drawing stares and attention from fascinated passers-by.

Designed by treehouse specialists, Baumraum, this egg-shaped room hovers high in the air in a northern German forest, giving its owners a private outdoor space for reading, napping or picnicking. The 10.6 square metre (34¾ sq ft) room is cantilevered from the trunk of a sturdy oak and braced by two V-shaped steel supports that hold it aloft almost six metres (19¾ ft). Like the supportive tree, the house is largely made of oak, wrapped with a curvaceous zinc roof and bookended by glossy white acrylic facades that emphasize its ovoid form. Guests enter the treehouse by climbing two ladders that pass through a generous open terrace, also of oak, and enter the modest white interior that includes built-in benches beside two large windows that survey the landscape beyond the tree canopy.

 Huddled between gabled sea huts, this 36 square metre (118 sq ft) holiday home draws on the form of its more traditional neighbours but reinterprets them in a contemporary manner. Almost entirely clad in cedar shingles, the main focus of the house is the sea view, which is framed by a full-height sliding glass panel that opens from the living room to the beach deck. The chalet is protected from flooding by galvanized steel stilts that also balance the slope of the plot and create space for a mezzanine sleeping platform at the rear. Simple plywood cladding is used throughout the interior, which houses a simple kitchen, bunk room, bathroom and a wood-burning stove.

| Project Name **Encuentro Guadalupe Ecoloft** | Location **Ensenada, Mexico** |
| Architect / Designer **Jorge Gracia** | Date **2011** |

 Part of a hotel, winery and restaurant in Mexico's viticulture region of Baja California, the distinctive accommodation at Encuentro Guadalupe includes twenty independent cabins, each held aloft from the rocky terrain by a steel frame. Envisaged as a harmonious addition to the landscape, the cabins are just 25 square metres (82 sq ft) but their elevated character gives soaring views across the valley. Each room opens to a private deck, which encourages guests to be in contact with their surroundings, albeit in a deluxe camping style. Clad with timber with Cor-Ten steel roofs, the material palette – like the structures themselves – is designed to blend seamlessly with the environment.

| Project Name **Garoza House 10.1** | Location **Ávila, Spain** |
| Architect / Designer **Herreros Arquitectos** | Date **2010** |

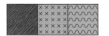 Providing a modest rural holiday home in a rugged Spanish landscape, this industrially-fabricated bolthole hovers lightly above its site, standing on slim steel legs anchored into the rocks below. Built off-site at a specialized factory, the prototypical house was produced from an amalgam of four basic prefabricated modules measuring just 3 × 2.5 metres (9¾ × 8¼ ft), which allows for future expansion and can be stacked vertically or horizontally, forming a building up to 12 metres (39¼ ft) long. The modules mean homes can be fabricated quickly and economically, and are easily hauled to site by conventional transport. The minimal building footprint and construction on the site help to preserve the ecological rhythm of the landscape while providing its owners an urban antidote.

Project Name **The Observatory**	Location **England, UK (or elsewhere)**
Architect / Designer **Feilden Clegg Bradley Studios**	Date **2015**

 In an effort to publicize the process of making art, this pair of charred wooden cabins, known collectively as The Observatory, was occupied by six artists-in-residence, and travelled across south England on the back of a flatbed truck. Designed by Lauren Shevills, Mina Gospavic, Ross Galtress and Charlotte Knight, with Edward Crumpton, the pair comprises The Workshop, a studio for the artist, and The Study, a more private place to eat, sleep and cook. Each is contained in an angular blackened timber body and mounted on a rotating base, which allows the artist to orientate the large picture window towards the most inspiring view. The same opening gives visitors a glimpse into how the artists work, highlighting the intention for the project to collapse the usual distinction between the rarefied art world and daily life.

Project Name	**House of Clothing**	Location	**Milan, Italy**
Architect / Designer	**MVRDV**	Date	**2008**

This prototype house by Dutch architects MVRDV was made from second-hand clothes sourced from Milan. The garments were packaged to create large blocks that were assembled around a steel frame, emulating the shape of a typical gabled home. Forming part of the 2008 Milan Triennale, with its inclusive theme of 'Casa Per Tutti' (Housing for All), invited architects were asked to design a basic shelter for those facing deprivation through environmental or social disorder. The project used recycled clothing – a readily available by-product of the fashion industry – and capitalized on its inherent properties of insulation. Each bundle of cloth was encased in a large clear plastic bag, which was wrapped with tape, securing the contents and displaying their texture and colour.

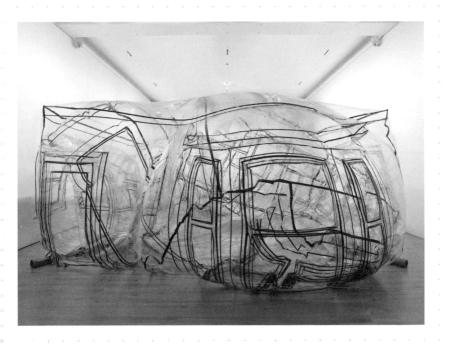

Schweder's inflatable artwork, *A Sac of Rooms All Day Long*, changes over time as its volumes inflate and deflate with air. This 'drawing' rendered in vinyl and air depicts the rooms of a larger house stuffed into the skin of a smaller one. Competing for limited space, the dining room steals space from the living room, which in turn steals space from the kitchen, and so on ... all day long. The rooms and their contents – stairs, cornices, windows and doors – are rendered onto the perimeter of the transparent house with black vinyl of varying thicknesses. This corresponds to the way architectural plans are drawn with different line weights to represent different elements. As the vinyl body inflates or deflates, visitors can see the coherence of the domestic arrangement with more or less clarity.

The Living Pavilion combines a pendulous timber frame, a grid of
437 recyclable plastic milk cartons and hundreds of shade-loving
plants to create an architectural pavilion that was installed on
Governor's Island in New York for one summer. Designed to evolve and grow through the
season, the living shady canopy was supported by plywood ribs that marched along its
9 metre (29½ ft) length and housed the plant-filled cartons, each secured with simple
plastic grating. On the upper side of the pavilion, sun-loving grass seed was sown to aid the
suspended plant's evaporative cooling process, known as evapotranspiration. Occasional
empty crates inside the green interior, drew light into the otherwise sheltered space.

Project Name **Triumph Pavilion**	Location **London, England, UK**
Architect / Designer **IPT Architects**	Date **2014**

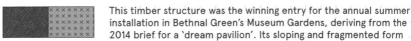

This timber structure was the winning entry for the annual summer installation in Bethnal Green's Museum Gardens, deriving from the 2014 brief for a 'dream pavilion'. Its sloping and fragmented form stands 4 metres (13 ft) tall at its peak and acts as a series of twelve frames, bookended by two sheltered polygonal boxes. As if carved apart by a giant hand, the triangulated frames serve to enclose and block views through the structure and around the park depending on the point of view. This encourages visitors to explore the effect of the form and linger on the matching oriented strand board (OSB) benches scattered nearby.

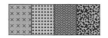 Part of ongoing research into form-finding at the University of Stuttgart, this folly results from an investigation by researchers who sought to translate natural lightweight structures into architectural form. The pavilion is based on the geometry of a beetle's wing case, known as *elytra*, and the double-layered folly of glass and carbon-fibre reinforced polymers is made up of thirty-six different geometric shapes. Robots were used to wind polymer fibres around custom-made steel frames to form the web-like modular components, which were then impregnated with resin for additional strength. The double-layered fibre composite structure minimized the amount of formwork while allowing geometric freedom: the dome spans 50 square metres (164 sq ft) but weighs only 593 kilograms (1307 lbs).

For fussy festivalgoers, the B-and-Bee sleeping cells are an ideal alternative to sharing a soggy tent. Constructed from a hexagonal larch structure, each compartment is large enough to contain a king-size bed and storage space, and is designed to be winched up onto an interlocking stack of accommodation, four units high, that could fit up to fifty music lovers within 100 square metres (328 sq ft) of ground. Including a locker, lighting and a power supply, the cells are enclosed by fabric covers that are sturdy enough to protect from the elements but can be propped open to aerate the space or for occupants to survey the scene. Upper rows of the compartments are accessed from a metal staircase that zigzags past the units below.

| Project Name | **Duel Nature** | Location | **Nevada, USA** |
| Artist / Designer | **Kate Raudenbush** | Date | **2006** |

Included in the 2006 Burning Man Festival and built in response to the given theme of 'Hope and Fear', the circular double-helix shape of Duel Nature alludes to the structure of DNA, the fundamental element of an organisms' chromosomes. Arranged in 120 fixed wing sets, each separated by a six-degree angle, the sculpture spans 12 metres (39¼ ft) and is held aloft by a circular steel frame around which the panels rotate. Each panel has a dual aspect: dull industrial plasma-cut steel clads the exterior wall of the piece while the interior face of the panels has a red mirrored finish, with red LED lights set into their tips.

| Project Name **Sam + Pam** | Location **Vancouver, Canada** | Date **2013** |

Architect / Designer **Office of McFarlane Biggar Architects + Designers**

This symmetrical structure by OMB responds to the brief for Canfor's Playhouse Challenge, an annual competition held to raise money for local causes. Using minimal materials for maximum fun, the two towers are shaped primarily by 50 × 75 millimetre (2 × 3 in) laths of timber that enclose three levels of platforms and create places to climb up, sit on or crawl through. Called Sam + Pam, the playful duo is linked by a red rope bridge and wooden monkey bars, and also includes a fireman's pole. Red-painted partitions within the towers demarcate smaller spaces and have cutout cartoon figures that children can climb through or play peek-a-boo inside.

Aligned with the seafront at La Grande Motte, this reflective, respiring pavilion was part of the annual Festival for Lively Architecture and was imagined by the architects as a transforming experience for visitors to the event. A slatted timber frame holds the dramatic main facade, which is composed of hundreds of lightweight mirrored panels, each suspended from rings that allow them to tilt and sway in the breeze. The hinged panels create a fluctuating mosaic of sea, sky and people's reflections as they explore the effect of the wind or playfully lift the flaps in a game of hide and seek.

Project Name **Floating Bath Pavilion**	Location **Søndre Havn, Denmark**
Architect / Designer **Rintala Eggertsson Architects**	Date **2012**

Commissioned for the outdoor exhibition 'Urban Play' in the city of Køge's Søndre Havn (South Harbour), the Floating Bath Pavilion by Rintala Eggertsson Architects was a part of eight artworks that responded to the industrial scale and materials of the area – one of Denmark's oldest harbours, which is undergoing urban redevelopment. The temporary timber pavilion was anchored at the end of the Søndre Havn jetty and provided a floating pontoon from which visitors could survey the horizon, dip their feet in the water – or bravely take a swim in the freezing waters and then warm up in the integrated fire-powered sauna afterwards.

 This hut for taking tea and meditating sits on four stilts and is characterized by its prominent V-shaped roof, which funnels rainfall into the adjacent pond. Slightly elevated and accessed by a shallow ramp, the hut is clad in cedar panels, punctuated with a full-height window that frames views of surrounding trees, and a narrow horizontal pane that faces the water. The hut provides a restful place from which to contemplate nature and emphasizes the effect of diurnal changes in light. Its plain white interior walls contrast with the small tea cabinet and glossy ebonized birch floor, which has a raised platform that holds three tatami mats.

| Project Name **Treehouse Riga** | Location **Azambuja, Portugal** |
| Architect / Designer **Appleton & Domingos** | Date **2010** |

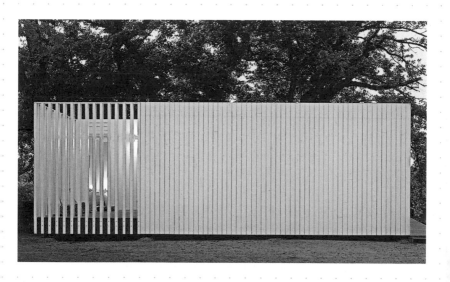

Responding to an increasing demand for compact and well-designed houses, Jular commissioned Appleton & Domingos to create the Treehouse Riga – a modular timber home of 22 square metres (72 sq ft), that includes basic domestic spaces for living, cooking, bathing and sleeping. Within the main living module, a large sliding birch door to the secondary bedroom can be retracted by day to increase the main living space, and closed for privacy at night. Similarly, full-height glazed doors open to two decks – positioned at opposite ends of the module – increase useable living space. Like the branches of a tree, the house is designed to grow vertically and horizontally in response to the changing needs of their inhabitants.

Project Name **Exbury Egg**	Location **Exbury, England, UK (or elsewhere)**
Architect / Designer **PAD Studio and Stephen Turner**	Date **2013**

Moored on an inlet of the Beaulieu River in Hampshire, the Egg is a workspace, home and laboratory for artist Stephen Turner. The self-sufficient oval structure is almost 6 metres (19¾ ft) long and is designed to act like a boat, rising and falling with the estuary's tides. It provides a place from which Turner can observe and collect data about the river that then informs his artworks. Constructed from two ovoid halves joined together, the boat uses traditional yacht-building techniques: Douglas Fir stringers secure the ribs of the Egg, which are cold moulded with narrow lengths of recycled cedar, coated with epoxy fibreglass to make it buoyant and stable. As well as a place to work, the project is a catalyst for an educational programme, intended to raise environmental awareness.

Commissioned by Emmy-winning musician Hans Liberg, this music studio by furniture designer Piet Hein Eek is a modern interpretation of a traditional rustic timber cabin located on the edge of a small forest. Embedded in the cross-section of a rectilinear pile of sawn logs, and in contrast to them, the blue-painted cabin interior contains seating, storage and tables for Liberg to work at. A band of windows at eye height punctures the wall of logs and frames views to the clearing and trees beyond. When closed, the window shutters are clad with log ends that carefully match the arrangement of stacked wood and disguise the studio within.

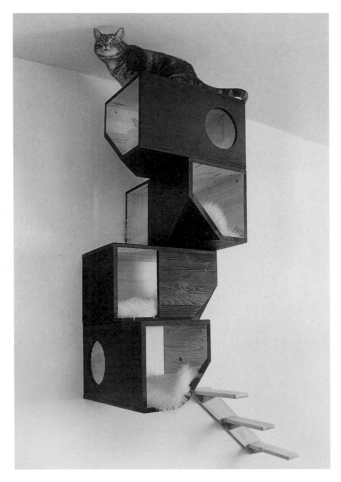

The Catissa, by Russian designer, Ilshat Garipov of Mojorno, offers an alternative view on housing for cats. Instead of cluttering floor space, Catissa is a wall-hung system for cats to sleep and hide in, high above the cacophony of most domestic spaces. Enclosed by five panels of timber, each of the 50 × 50 centimetre (19¾ in) cubes can be stacked above each other and have cut-out windows and feline-sized gaps, providing multiple places for cats to spy from and slink through. Detachable sheepskin cushions and a diminutive cat-ladder complete the design, which is available in monochrome or colourful painted hues.

Project Name **Signal Ethique**	Location **Puy de Dôme, Sancy, France**
Architect / Designer **Arnaud Huart**	Date **2014**

Sitting atop the dormant volcano of Puy de Dôme, part of the French Massif Central, this timber tower is a small refuge for rest and contemplation, and humbly echoes the temples that once stood on this site. The volanic, layered geography of the surrounding landscape is referenced by the tower's construction, which is formed of sheets of board separated by timber beams. A band of open cells in the upper quarter of the 4.7 metre (15½ ft) high building allows daylight and air to enter the small space; by night it acts as a beacon with electric light streaming out from the interior.

Project Name **Woodpile**	Location **Winnipeg, Canada**	
Architect / Designer **Talmon Biran Architecture Studio**		Date **2011**

Part of the annual competition for Warming Huts along the Assiniboine River in Winnipeg, this mutable design by Noa Biran and Roy Talmon responds to the changing needs of skiers as winter temperatures give way to spring. Enclosed by a mesh of steel that surrounds a central fireplace, the walls also create shelving for stacked firewood and are piled high as winter approaches. Providing fuel for the fire and shelter from icy gales, the walls slowly diminish in size as the season passes and the wood is burned, providing a bright and warming shelter for skiers. As warmer weather approaches, the interior is gradually revealed as a simple rectilinear pavilion, entirely open to the elements.

Project Name **Final Wooden House**	Location **Kumamoto, Japan**
Architect / Designer **Sou Fujimoto**	Date **2008**

Like an over-scaled version of the children's game, Jenga, the Final Wooden House is composed of hundreds of evenly sized square profile cedar beams 35 square centimetres (15¾ sq ft). Japanese architect Sou Fujimoto's design was intended to exploit the diverse uses of timber and the identical components are simply stacked atop each other to create an interlocking tower. Floors, walls, roof, structure, furniture and seating are all formed from the same material and can morph from one function to another, depending on how visitors move through the interior and use the space. Surrounded by forest, the simplicity of the design also encourages quiet contemplation of the natural environment.

Project Name **Santa Monica Bus Shelters**	Location **Santa Monica, California, USA**
Architect / Designer **Lorcan O'Herlihy Architects**	Date **2014**

These modular bright blue bus shelters are the result of a commission from Los Angeles City Council to revive the reputation of its ailing public transport network. The distinctive blue steel discs are mounted on slim columns and overlap each other; their flexible configuration accommodates a range of sizes, locations and shading necessary for the 360 different bus stops. Below the blue canopy, simple circular stools are fixed to the concrete, and echo the colour and shapes overhead. Though the discs may appear to be a deceptively simple solution, they carefully take account of the warm Californian climate, resistance to vandalism and maximum visibility for passengers' safety.

Project Name **Moving Icon**		Location **Westphalia, Germany (or elsewhere)**
Architect / Designer **Kalhöfer Korschildgen**		Date **2013**

Marked by its white gabled roof mounted on a transportable platform, Moving Icon is a mobile information centre designed to communicate the architecture of historic cities through digital and printed media. Housed in an archetypal gabled form that typifies regional housing, the project is designed to be easily set up and demounted, towed from village to village by car. Its hinged walls fold down and outward to become signboards, awnings and ramps, while the translucent gabled shell becomes a beacon at night, broadcasting thematic words that advertise the nature of the project and draw members of the public to discover the information held within.

Project Name **Walden**		Location **Germany**	
Architect / Designer **Nils Holger Moorman**			Date **2006**

Conceived in the spirit of Henry David Thoreau's novel, *Walden: Or, Life in the Woods*, this project by furniture designer Nils Holger Moorman, is a place to enjoy spending time outdoors in nature. The oversized shed is clad in vertical strips of timber, with special niches cut out on each side for garden tools, as well as for a large fire cauldron, firewood stack, retractable eaves to protect against sun and rain, and even a birdhouse. Cut out of the centre of Walden is a two-seater booth for resting, reading or entertaining, cloaked by a red curtain. Another niche holds a narrow ladder that leads to a sunroof.

Project Name **Genesis**	Location **Miami, Florida, USA**
Architect / Designer **Adjaye Associates**	Date **2011**

Designed as an immersive visitor experience at the entrance to the 2011 Design Miami show, Genesis is a temporary pavilion composed of two interlocking timber frames that combine structure, seating, windows and doors. The frames form a triangular prism that is pared away at the centre to form the shape of a large ovoid. The angle and aperture of the single hole punctures all sides of the prism, creating an entry, exit, window and light well. Within the oval interior, a secondary layer of timber frames carved at seat-height form integrated benches for visitors to rest, gather and take in framed views of galleries beyond. Spaces between the timber frames allow light to filter through the gaps, creating a dappled effect.

Project Name **Mi Casa, Your Casa**	Location **Atlanta, Georgia, USA**
Architect / Designer **Esrawe + Cadena**	Date **2014**

Rather than being a stark untouchable exhibit, the impetus behind *Mi Casa, Your Casa* was to encourage people to interact with each other. In particular, the installation referenced the lively human behaviour seen at daily street markets in Latin America. Forty miniature houses, each identical in size in shape, outline the typical and recognizable shape of a house. The red-painted steel frames were each slung with a hammock and arranged in low-rise rows on the lawn, in contrast to the large white museum buildings towering behind. The diminutive scale and familiar shape of the homes were intended to encourage the local community to relax and use the space as if it were their own home: a place for playing, picnicking, resting, eating and talking.

| Project Name | **Embedded Project** | | Location | **Shanghai, China** |
| Architect / Designer | **HHD_FUN** | | Date | **2009** |

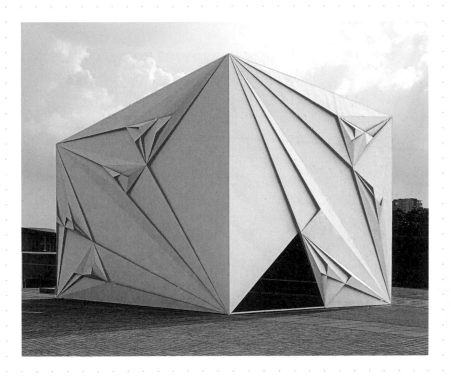

Part of the 2010 Expo, Embedded Project is an experiment in surface form by HHD_FUN that is based on a triangular fractal pattern, which results in an amalgam of subdivided triangles. Computational algorithms were used as a method to organize the 'cracked' panels, which range in scale from one large triangular base, to dozens of smaller interlocking folded planes, each marked by a raised surface and outlined in fluorescent pink paint. Built in just five days, the plain white internal timber walls of the 100 square metre (328 sq ft) pavilion were used to project a film by the artist, Xu Wenkai.

| Project Name **Dragon Skin Pavilion** | Location **Hong Kong, China** | Date **2012** |

Architect / Designer **LEAD and EDGE Laboratory for Architectural and Urban Research**

Included as part of the 2011-2012 Hong Kong and Shenzhen Bi-City Biennale, this modular timber structure is an exploration into the potential of digital design and fabrication processes, using materials as efficiently as possible. The arched structure is created from 163 pieces of post-formable plywood. Each piece was cut to a unique shape and formed using a single mould, interlocking with its neighbouring pieces to create a stacked, three-dimensional shell. Secured without the aid of glue, nails or other adhesives, Dragon Skin Pavilion is self-supporting – its lightweight form and unusual shape create apertures in a striking lattice, filtering light inward or projecting it out depending on the time of day.

Project Name **ArboSkin Pavilion**	Location **Stuttgart, Germany**
Architect / Designer **University of Stuttgart ITKE**	Date **2013**

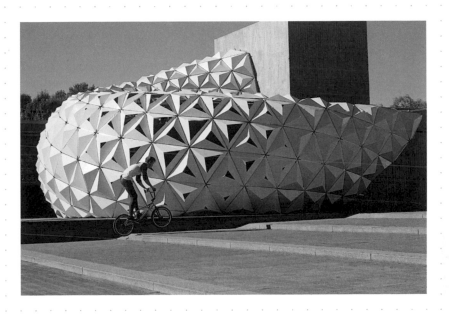

This double-curved pavilion by ITKE at Stuttgart University illustrates the structural properties of bioplastics developed specifically for use in the construction industry. Each of the pavilion modules is thermo-formed into a pyramidal shape from a flat sheet of bioplastic granules, some of which were trimmed with CNC milling to remove greater or lesser amounts of the triangular point, thereby creating apertures. The temporary pavilion's load-bearing walls are formed of modules linked by bracing rings and joists. Because the modules are made of a renewable biomass, the shelter can simply be composted when no longer needed.

| Project Name **Swoosh Pavilion** | Location **London, England, UK** | |
| Architect / Designer **Architectural Association School of Architecture** | | Date **2008** |

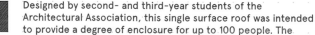

Designed by second- and third-year students of the
Architectural Association, this single surface roof was intended
to provide a degree of enclosure for up to 100 people. The
6 metre (19¾ ft) wide project wraps around a central lamppost and unfurls from this
central fulcrum in a series of curving vertical columns. Assembled from 653 pieces
of laminated timber veneer, each of the columns is connected by short beams that
decrease in height and density as they spiral away from the centre. The lowest edges of
Swoosh become low benches that encourage people to sit and meet informally, take
their lunch or just rest beneath the wooden canopy.

| Project Name **The Pinch** | Location **Shuanghe, Yunnan Province, China** |
| Architect / Designer **John Lin and Olivier Ottevaere** | Date **2014** |

Designed and built by John Lin and Olivier Ottevaere with a team of Hong Kong University students, this library and community centre provides a significant public facility for the earthquake-damaged town. Nicknamed The Pinch, the project is constructed from wooden planks that extend over the roof of the library and reach the ground, allowing people to walk across the slope. Its gentle sweeping surface means children can use it as a playground and it also acts as bleachers for the basketball court below. Inside, timber trusses support hanging wooden bookshelves and cladding of polycarbonate panels, which allows daylight to flood the space.

Project Name **Crazy Hyperculture in the Vertigo of the World**	Location **Buenos Aires, Argentina**
Artist / Designer **Ernesto Neto**	Date **2011**

Suspended above the floor of Faena Arts Centre, this interactive work by Ernesto Neto is a labyrinth of colourful netting that allows visitors to traverse through its core on undulating sky roads. The inhabitable web can be entered from two ramps, which lead into the belly of the circuitous path, passing through clusters of spices of various colours and scent that amplify the visitor's sense of smell, as well as balance, since the sculpture sways in response to each person's weight and movement. The sky roads are held aloft from the rafters by reinforced netting and held taut by the weight of the webbed labyrinth.

Housing a venue for concerts, presentations and gatherings on the Detmold University campus, the curvaceous yellow and red surface of Boxel designed by Henri Schweynoch was the winning project for a full scale pavilion designed as part of the university's Digital Design course. The parametrically-designed pavilion has a surprisingly pragmatic building material at its heart – more than 2,000 beer crates donated from a local brewery were used to make the project. The boxes are organized next to each other and secured with invisible slat and screw fixings. Its final shape and structural performance were analyzed using parametric software, which finessed the position and curves to gain maximum strength with a minimum surface area.

| Project Name **Park(ing) Day** | Location **San Francisco, California, USA** | Date **2011** |

Architect / Designer **Studios Architecture, Chris Chalmers, Holmes-Culley Engineers**

This car-inspired pavilion was designed for PARK(ing) day, an annual international event for artists, designers and citizens to transform car parking spaces into temporary public 'parks'. Formed from more than 250 large-format cardboard printer rolls, and connected by 160 CNC-cut MDF joints, the pavilion provides a space to recline in the shape of a compact SUV – sculpted out of a rectilinear grid of cardboard tubes that fills the parking space. A collaboration between Studios Architecture, Chris Chalmers and Holmes-Culley Engineers, the pavilion was assembled without fasteners or glue, to allow for both ease of construction and to create a design that can be fully recycled.

Project Name **Newton's Cottage**	Location **London, England, UK**
Architect / Designer **Observatorium**	Date **2014**

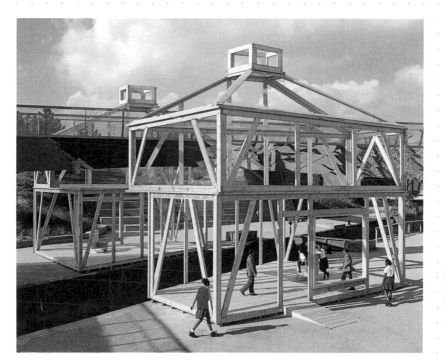

Formed of two timbered halves that straddle a lock and mirrored bridge, this temporary events pavilion, called Newton's Cottage, frames the Carpenters Road Lock on the River Lea. Designed by the Dutch art collective Observatorium, the wooden frame delineates the shape of a former 1930s lock-keeper's cottage, which formerly stood on the site. Newton's Cottage is named for the last lock keeper in residence, and has been used to host events and activities to communicate the history of the lock. Its materiality is an inherent part of this: the area was once part of a timber yard and this contemporary folly was built in collaboration with students at the local Building Crafts College, which continues to teach a wide range of traditional crafts techniques.

| Project Name **Pallet House** | Location **Oberstdorf, Germany** |
| Architect / Designer **Matthias Loebermann** | Date **2005** |

A temporary meeting place for the World Ski Championships in Oberstdorf, the Pallet House creates an architectural pavilion that expresses timber in a fully sustainable way. Using common shipping pallets as a modular structural unit that was easily found, the pavilion could be completely dissembled and recycled when no longer needed. Arranged in a curvilinear form, the 1,300 stacked pallets are anchored by twenty tie rods fixed into the ground, and secured with straps at regular intervals for stability. The pallet structure creates an alternating wall of open and closed spaces, which allows light to filter in through a sinuous grid. At night, interior light projects through the gaps and draws people inside.

Project Name **SEAT Public Pavilion**	Location **Georgia, USA**
Architect / Designer **E/B Office**	Date **2012**

A winning entry of the Flux Project in Atlanta's Freedom Park, the SEAT Public Pavilion is formed of 400 IKEA timber seats that rise and fall in accord with the mathematical pattern of a sine wave. Designed by E/B Office as a way to reconsider the fundamental act of sitting – and the relation between a seat and architectural space – the cantilevered chairs rise from two concrete bases and were assembled via an additive process. Beginning at the edges and corners and filling in the arched form, the chairs were attached with carefully hidden lag bolts, clamps and screws to create an ambiguous folly. Chairs around the periphery are slightly rotated to allow visitors to face the city and landscape; in contrast, the inward-facing chairs at the base of the pavilion provide a sheltered intimate zone.

Project Name **Glass House**	Location **Milan, Italy**
Architect / Designer **Santambrogiomilano**	Date **2012**

In the grand modernist tradition of Philip Johnson's Glass House (1949) or Mies van der Rohe's Farnsworth House (1951), this house of glass by Italian architect, Carlo Santambrogio, manifests the idea of living in a forest, rather than a house. Its translucent walls of structural and double-glazed panes are intended to provide the least intrusive layer between nature and man, providing shelter and amenity without filtering out the view, light, sound or inhabitants of a natural forest environment. Arranged over three floors, with all structure, circulation and interior divisions rendered in glass, guests can survey 360-degree views inside this gleaming house among the trees.

 This twenty-first-century version of the Fly's Eye Dome commissioned by The Buckminster Fuller Institute reworks Fuller's original design, first patented in 1965. The 7.3 metre (24 ft) high structure marks Palm Court in Miami's Design District and is formed from contemporary materials and techniques that improve on the strength and durability of Fuller's earlier fibreglass prototype. Fabricated by Goetz Composites and Bruce Marek, the parametrically-designed, composite structure was milled with CNC machines to create moulds for the modular units. The dome holds dozens of high-impact acrylite lenses in place and, in accordance with Fuller's intent to maximize the sustainability of his 'autonomous dwelling machines', it collects rainwater run-off.

Project Name **Read Nest**		Location **Northern Zealand, Denmark**
Architect / Designer **Dorte Mandrup Arkitekter**		Date **2008**

This holiday home in Northern Zealand was designed as a private cabin in which to read, rest or work. Providing just 9.8 square metres (32 sq ft) of space, the singular hut is a basic amalgam of just one large window, one rooflight, one door, one bed, one desk and a single wall of shelving – the minimum shelter, light and furniture required for a simple place of respite. Though spartan, each element of the interior is carefully considered for its purpose: the desk looks out to a view from the window, books and other equipment can be stored in the full-height shelves and the bed is elevated in the rear of the cabin, bathed in daylight filtered by the clerestory window.

| Project Name | **Chapel St Geneviève** | Location | **Saint-Maurice-sous-les-Côtes, France** |
| Architect / Designer | **OBIKA Architecture** | Date | **2014** |

Situated in the natural park of Lorraine and surrounded by woodland, this small chapel replaces an existing structure that was damaged by fire. Its simple timber framework echoes the forested context and emulates the original form and scale of the chapel. In essence, the project is constructed from modular timber trusses, which were prefabricated then installed on site. The trusses are placed along the building at regular half-metre (1½ ft) intervals, visually linking the chapel, altar and refuge, which houses a range of activities for exhibitions, readings and performances – or simply provides shelter for hikers using the popular trails around the site.

Project Name **Roman Villa**	Location **Brederis, Austria**	
Architect / Designer **Marte.Marte Architekten**	Date **2008**	

 Marking the remains of a Roman settlement in Austria's Feldkirch area, this 42 square metre (137¾ sq ft) Cor-Ten steel sculpture sits between the stone foundations of two different Roman villas, creating a place from which to contemplate the two house types. The Cor-Ten tower stands almost 10 metres (32¾ ft) high and acts as a suitably rusted beacon for the site. It encases a portion of the stone foundations below, which are revealed through glazed incisions punched into the side and base of the steel volume. A trapezoid-shaped platform also made of Cor-Ten extends from the tower and continues the datum of the stone remains. Partially shielded by a 3 metre (9¾ ft) high wall, one of the platform edges displays items inset in protected niches.

| Project Name **Flake House** | Location **Frossay, France (or elsewhere)** |
| Architect / Designer **Olgga** | Date **2006** |

Known as Flake House, this architectural interpretation of a broken tree branch was designed for the French competition 'Small Machines to Live In' held by CAUE 72. The pair of wooden, prefabricated cabins is clad with rough-sawn half logs, like a traditional ski chalet, and the rudimentary exteriors contrast with the smoothly finished plywood walls inside. Providing just 22 square metres (72 sq ft) of space, the cabins crack apart, housing living and dining areas in one half, and bathing in the other. The junction where the cabins split and visitors enter is studded with log ends cut at irregular depths to create a rugged textural entrance wall – in contrast to the fully glazed facing walls that frame bucolic views to the Loire. Both cabins are proportioned for transportation by truck.

 Based on the observation that a shadow could be understood as an entire three-dimensional shape, this conceptual installation by Michael Jantzen is a playful optical puzzle that renders a temporal experience concrete. The artist recorded shadows cast from a modelled traditional cottage at a specific time and date then built the outline at full scale from timber. The shadows are recast as a three-dimensional record of the moment: the body of the house fades into a tapered black volume, which appears ephemeral from far away and surprisingly solid up close. This conceit is reinforced by the distorted shape and shadowing of stairs and windows.

| Project Name **Parasite** | Location **Rotterdam, The Netherlands** |
| Architect / Designer **Korteknie Stuhlmacher Architecten** | Date **2001** |

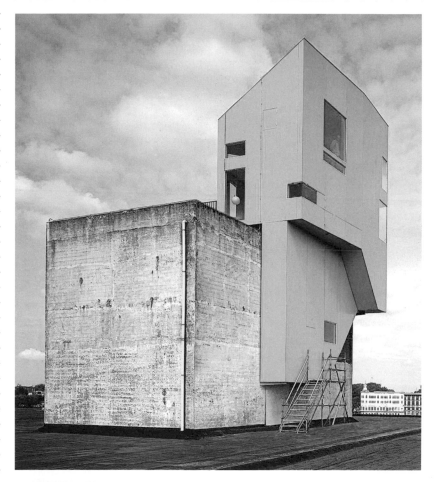

This parasitic addition to Rotterdam's skyline formed part of the city's celebrations in its year as Europe's Cultural Capital in 2001. Clasped onto the elevator shaft of the former Las Palmas warehouse building, the distinctive green exterior of this prototypical house was constructed from solid laminated timber panels cut to size off-site and assembled in only a few days. Containing simple living, sleeping and bathing rooms, the proportions and weight of Parasite were designed to be fully supported by the shaft. Interior plywood surfaces are unpainted and pre-fabricated windows and shutters of varying sizes were inserted into the form, giving lofty views across the city.

| Project Name **Mizoën Information Point** | Location **Mizoën, France** |
| Architect / Designer **Hérault Arnod Architectes** | Date **1995** |

Standing beside the national highway not far from Grenoble, this rusted information point is an unusual contrast to usual French visitor chalets. The 20 square metre (65½ sq ft) Cor-Ten steel structure is built vertically, to maximize use of the narrow site, which is wedged between a towering rocky cliff and the large Chambon Lake Dam below. Embedded into the rock and with a skin rusted like the iron oxide found in local rocks, the project makes reference to its surroundings but its orthogonal form also contrasts with the jagged Alpine scenery. Visitors ascend a narrow staircase to reach the protected viewing point, which looks over the dam and mountainous landscape.

Project Name **BCN Re.set Identity Pavilion**	Architect / Designer **Urbanus**
Location **Barcelona, Spain**	Date **2014**

Extending from a section of ancient Roman wall in Barcelona's Plaça Nova, this installation responds to the festival theme of 'Identity' with a bamboo lattice that mimics the shape and scale of ancient Roman and Catalan vaults. Constructed from a porous grid of 10 millimetres (½ in) thick bamboo, the two types of arches illustrate structural and historical progression and are arranged with the Roman arches along one side, facing the larger single Catalan vault. Designed for the annual BCN Re.Set event, the self-supporting structure acted as a visually arresting meeting point for visitors.

| Project Name **Colonnade I** | Location **London, England, UK** | Date **2013** |

Architect / Designer **Lucie Beauvert and Paol Kemp with Johanna Nocke**

Responding to the surrounding context of a disused industrial building in South London, Colonnade I is a collaboration created by textile designer Lucie Beauvert and architect Paol Kemp, and developed with Johanna Nocke. The project marks the perimeter of eight columns, made of hundreds of metres of thread and suspended from a textile framework tensioned by bags of cast concrete. The spectre of red columns is secured to the concrete below and allows people to pass through the delicate passage of pillars, which appear to shift perspective depending on the visitor's point of view, forming a spectral contrast to the robust brick walls of the factory.

| Project Name | The Strange Loop You Are | Location | Jerusalem, Israel |
| Artists | Mike and Doug Starn | Date | 2015 |

This is the ninth iteration of the Starn brothers' Big Bambú installation works, which have been shown worldwide. Entitled *The Strange Loop You Are*, this complex piece took the brothers and their team of rock climbers more than a month to construct using 10,000 bamboo lengths bound by rope. The structure stands 16 metres (52½ ft) tall and is composed of a labyrinth of bamboo spears that meander across part of the Billy Rose Art Garden in the Israel Museum. While the finished product gives visitors far-reaching views of Jerusalem, the construction process was also part of the project, allowing people to understand the demanding techniques used to make it.

 Standing three storeys above the water, this tower for officials to observe the finish line of annual regattas on Lake Rotsee is opened only three weeks each year and the design responds to this infrequency of use. Conceived as a dynamic sculptural building, the hardy prefabricated pine construction hovers above the water on a pillared concrete platform. Its large-scale shutters can transform the tower, to slide open or fold up when in use but are otherwise closed and protect all sides of the building. As the tower is prominently located in a picturesque setting, the shutters create sculptural relief on the facade and cast variegated shadows that reduce its apparent mass.

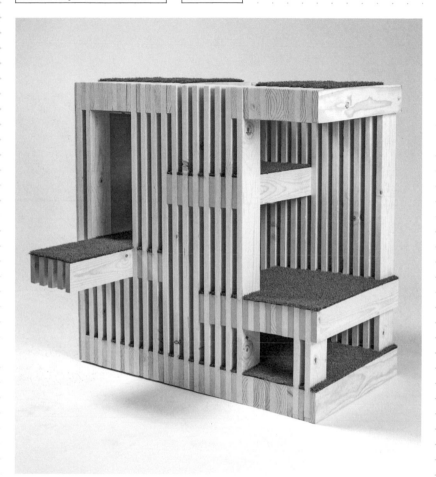

Kitty Condo was contributed as part of a fundraising event organized by Architects for Animals in aid of the Los Angeles-based charity, FixNation, which rescues and spays feral cats. Designed by RNL Architects, the five-level cat apartment provided a sheltered place for cats to hide in and survey the world from. Screened by parallel walls formed of twenty-three vertical timber slats, the condo is essentially a series of platforms enclosed by, or cantilevered from, the wooden structure, each lined with artificial grass. The design mimics typical American residential arrangements of small, stacked apartment blocks with balconies, and is a playful response to the original brief for a cat shelter.

| Project Name **Hermès Rive Gauche** | Location **Paris, France** |
| Architect / Designer **RDAI** | Date **2010** |

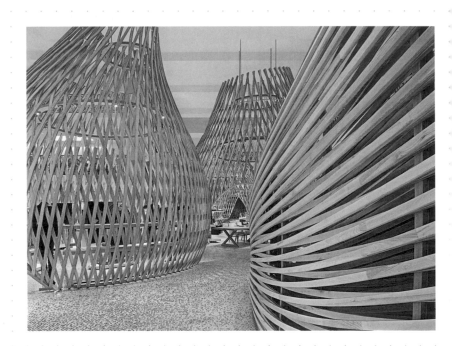

 Occupying what was once the Art Deco Lutétia swimming pool in St. Germain, this new Parisian boutique for Hermés is marked by three timber pavilions, each 9 metres (29¾ ft) high, that house collections of the celebrated French fashion house. The self-supporting structures are formed of ash laths with a 60 × 40 millimetre (2¼ × 1½ in) profile woven together with a double radius curvature that gives the bulb-like pavilions a slight lean. With a shape that is redolent of a Weaver bird's nest, each of the latticed wood vaults stand almost three storeys tall and create a focal point for shoppers in the lofty pale space. A lower wooden structure also of ash wraps the staircase in similar latticework and leads from the pavilions to upper levels of the boutique.

Project Name	Galaxies Forming Along Filaments, Like Droplets Along the Strands of A Spider's Web
Artist / Designer **Tomás Saraceno**	Location **Venice, Italy** · Date **2009**

Fascinated by large-scale studies of the universe, and the discovery of its sponge-like structure – with galaxies formed along filaments – artist and architect Tomás Saraceno created an installation that illustrates this effect. Drawing a parallel between galactic filaments and a spider's web, the piece is constructed from interwoven elastic rope that stretches between walls, floors and ceilings, intersecting to form a dense central cluster. Appearing like over-scaled molecules, the radiating ropes force visitors to interact with the work as they weave under, around or over the webs to pass through the room. Accidental collisions affect all parts of the structure, exactly as it does for spiders and galaxies.

MICRO

MINI

MIDI

MACRO

MAXI

Designed by Irish architects Hall McKnight as part of the 2015 London Festival of Architecture, this primrose-yellow pavilion houses a library of 1,000 bricks, all sourced from a single street in Belfast. Installed in Cubitt Square at Kings Cross and supported by Irish Design 2015, the pavilion's three-storey facade is marked by arches incized into angled panels that reference the historic rail viaducts nearby. The slim arcades also act to highlight the display of bricks inside. Re-appropriated from a terraced street, the bricks are analogous with the festival's theme of 'Work in Progress' - each humble element being one part of a greater whole, just as a city is.

Linking two school playgrounds previously separated by a change in level, this brightly coloured canopy of folded 10 millimetre (¼ in) thick steel sheet is a simple solution that provides protection from the elements as well as a new identity for the school. In contrast to the typically white-washed walls of the 'pueblo blanco' village this structure is painted turquoise on the upper side, and fuchsia pink underneath. The striking angular form draws on techniques of origami to create an integrated structure and roof surface, and also encloses a new ramp and staircase.

| Project Name **Bergen Safe House** | Location **Bergen, Norway** |
| Architect / Designer **Max Rink, Rachel Griffin, Simon de Jong** | Date **2012** |

Standing as a monument to the fiery history of Bergen city, which has been razed sixteen times in the last 800 years, the Bergen Safe House was designed and built in just four days for a local competition. Embodying the dyadic human relationship to fire as both an element of warmth and of destruction, the tower is made from 50 × 50 millimetre (2 × 2 in) timber beams that are blackly scorched on the exterior but remain unblemished on the inside. Emulating the Japanese technique of *shou sugi ban*, the charcoal facade protects the structure from further decay by fire or insects. Inside, the three-storey-tall Safe House has multi-level platforms that can accommodate sleeping, working or socialising.

| Project Name **One Man Sauna** | Location **Bochum, Germany** |
| Architect / Designer **Modulorbeat** | Date **2014** |

Rising up from an abandoned factory site on the outskirts of Bochum, the One Man Sauna is a temporary tower that stands 7.5 metres (24½ ft) tall and contains a series of rooms for personal relaxation. Formed of precast concrete frames that were sourced from a old shaft mine building, the sauna includes a plunge pool at the lower level, a one-man sauna lined with plywood in the middle, and a small deck for resting above. At the top a roof light can be opened to reveal views to the deserted surroundings. Accessed by a ladder of steel treads that are stapled into the concrete from ground level, the sauna is part of Modulorbeat's investigations into the use of marginalized places in Bochum city.

Project Name **Parasite Pavilion**	Location **Venice, Italy**	
Architect / Designer **Pier Alessio Rizzardi/TCA Think Tank**	Date **2014**	

 This sinuous passage of plastic and steel was the result of an intensive, five-day 'bug dome' workshop at the Venice Biennale, providing a direct architectural experience for visitors and offering them a shaded place to rest between the lively cultural events of Giardini and Arsenale. Formed of large-scale arches secured at regular intervals into a non-woven textile base, the tunnel shape was delineated by layers of PVC tubing woven through the framework. As well as providing structural reinforcement, the tubes lead visitors through the tunnel, which has a girth that compresses and expands according to the geometry of two guiding curves and the related proximity to Biennale buildings and entrances.

Project Name **Salzburg Pavilion**	Location **Salzburg, Austria**
Architect / Designer **Soma Architecture**	Date **2011**

The State of Salzburg commissioned this temporary pavilion for use during the city's renowned annual festival of music. Like a highly polished web of silvery sticks, the pavilion is formed of individual aluminium profiles cut to a uniform length that are held apart from each other by cylindrical sections of tubing. Hundreds of aluminium pieces are amassed to form the arcing tunnel that can be used every year to host concerts, events or presentations for the festival. From afar, the glistening but indecipherable form of the pavilion provokes interest and draws visitors to explore the project further; the form and construction of its amorphous body becomes clear on closer inspection.

Designed to celebrate the All Souls Day Festival in the Netherlands, this inflatable picnic pavilion centres on the wood-burning stove, which was used to cook hot food and drinks as well as to heat the air that fills the pillowy canopy. Providing shelter for the picnickers below, the roof is held aloft by six elongated timber trestles that are integrated into the pair of long tables and can seat up to forty people. At night, the roof is illuminated, acting as a beacon for the celebratory event and lighting the table and stove beneath.

Project Name **Delirious Frites**	Location **Quebec, Canada**
Architect / Designer **Les Astronautes**	Date **2014**

Squeezed between the walls of a historic passage in Quebec, Delirious Frites is a temporary installation composed of hundreds of swimming pool noodles, or *frites de piscine*, waving from the walls. The mass of pink and orange noodles is part of a public art festival called Les Passages Insolites that awarded Les Astronautes the project to revitalize a forgotten part of the city. Affixed to tall, pink painted wall panels, the *frites* of soft foam gently bowed under their own weight, almost meeting in the middle but allowing just enough room for visitors to pass through or hide within.

| Project Name **String Vienna** | Location **Vienna, Austria** |
| Architect / Designer **Numen/For Use** | Date **2014** |

 String Vienna is the latest exploration by the design collective Numen/For Use that transforms simple materials into fantastic experiences – this time turning a load of hot air into an acrobatic internal climbing frame. Encased by a large white envelope of reinforced foil and high strength polyester coated in polyurethane, the self-supporting sculpture looks like a purist bouncy castle from the outside. Within, however, hundreds of parallel blue climbing ropes attached to the interior are connected in a grid formation. When inflated, the envelope expands, creating tension on the ropes so they rise and create a three-dimensional grid that is strong enough to support the weight of climbers. Within, the encompassing inflated white interior forms an illusory scale-less background.

| Project Name **Peace Pavilion** | Location **London, England, UK** |
| Architect / Designer **Atelier Zündel Cristea** | Date **2013** |

Peace Pavilion is an inflated PVC membrane formed from a topological deformation of a torus – the prize-winning entry for a competition sponsored by ArchTriumph for a summer pavilion in London's Bethnal Green. The 62 square metre (203½ sq ft) project is a self-supporting structure bound by a continuous, undulating tube of inflated air that rests at three points on an anodized aluminium platform. A clear plastic sheet spans the interior space and is zipped to the inflated white frame. Visitors were invited to explore the striking toroidal structure, including its bouncy roof that children could climb across from one of the structure's resting points. Generated mathematically, the symmetrical shape was intended to convey a state of peaceful equilibrium.

Project Name **Bränden Bus Stop**	Location **Krumbach, Austria**
Architect / Designer **Sou Fujimoto**	Date **2014**

Sou Fujimoto's Bränden Bus Stop substitutes a traditional covered bus shelter for a clustered 'wood' of slim steel rods at the roadside. An open wooden staircase winds up through the rods, allowing passengers and passers-by the chance to climb up the precarious treads to survey panoramic views of Krumbach. The striking forest of white-painted steel references the natural wooded surroundings and also functions as a landmark that draws people to meet and converse there, whether waiting for a bus or not. Though it offers negligible protection from the elements, the design provokes a new way to contemplate how we use places and their relation to nature.

 Formed of a honeycomb structure, Softwall is an expandable system that allows rooms to be divided and enclosed by the freestanding paper wall it swells to create. Designed by Canadian architects Stephanie Forsythe and Todd MacAllen, the wall continues their exploration into how smaller and tactile objects can shape how we experience larger spaces. Secured by concealed magnetic fasteners, Softwalls are manufactured in varying heights and allow users to stack together or extend the length of each unit to create rooms as large or small as needed. The impact of different materials - textile, kraft paper or tissue – also controls the amount of light filtered into the miniature rooms through opaque or diffuse surfaces.

Project Name	The New Summerhouse	Location	London, England, UK
Architect / Designer	Ullmayer Sylvester Architects	Date	2004

 Inserted at the rear of a Victorian terrace in London, the function of this reflective summerhouse includes a wide range of activities for a young family. The 8 metre (26¼ ft) long shed is both painter's studio, garden shed, table tennis venue and a place for children's sleepovers, giving the growing family enough extra room to stay in their small property. The modest summerhouse has a timber frame clad internally with birch-faced plywood and enclosed by lightweight polycarbonate sheets and a dog-legged wall of polished stainless steel that bounces light into the garden, reflects the foliage and flowers, and amplifies the sense of being enveloped in a private retreat.

| Project Name **Archive Artist's Pavilion** | Location **Amsterdam, The Netherlands** |
| Architect / Designer **Bureau LADA** | Date **2008** |

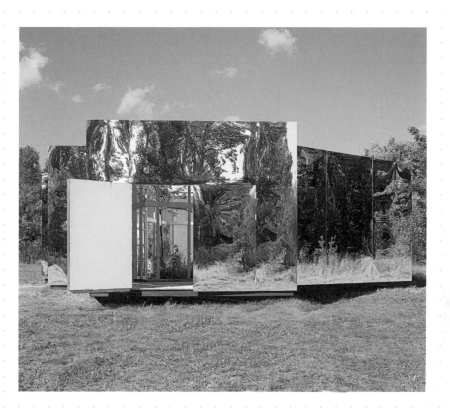

 Imagined as an innovative and functional archive space for a contemporary artist, this pavilion was constructed at the Dutch artist's centre Nieuw en Meer as part of the Atelier Malkovich ideas competition. One of eight pavilions built, Archive is essentially a wooden corridor, enclosed by semi-translucent panels on the inside, and camouflaged from the outside by mirrors. These highly reflective surfaces mimic the surrounding garden and pique visitor's interest in the pavilion. A small gap in the facade allows them a glimpse of the interior, which is fitted with wooden shelves and pegs that recall Shaker hooks and are designed to hold the artist's materials and objects of inspiration. The corridor opens to a small inner garden – the green heart of the studio.

Project Name **Endless Stair**	Location **London, England, UK**
Architect / Designer **dRMM Architects**	Date **2013**

An amalgam of fifteen staircases, Endless Stair by dRMM was installed on the lawns of Tate Modern as part of London Design Week. Creating an illusory optical punch, the combined stairways are constructed from offcuts of cross-laminated panels of tulipwood timber normally used for skirting boards. Though optically beguiling, visitors could actually climb up, down and beneath the structure that gave elevated views across the River Thames to St. Paul's Cathedral. As in daily life, the stairs created places for people to meet, cross over and converse – some leading from one to the next, others like a dead-end maze, and all threaded with timber hand rails the depth of stair treads, which further emphasized the visual misperception.

| Project Name | High Views, Boston Pendulum | Location | Lincolnshire, England, UK |
| Architect / Designer | Robbrecht en Daem | Date | 2007 |

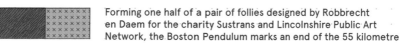 Forming one half of a pair of follies designed by Robbrecht en Daem for the charity Sustrans and Lincolnshire Public Art Network, the Boston Pendulum marks an end of the 55 kilometre (34 mi) cycle path that runs along the Witham River between Boston and Lincoln. The staircase appears to cantilever precariously over the path. Its steel structure is clad with strips of larch mounted in even intervals to the frame – the narrow gaps giving glimpses through the lookout. Occasionally painted in strips of red, white or blue, the larch laths also reference the coloured feathers of local birds. From the uppermost point, visitors survey a broad expanse of the flat Lincolnshire Fens landscape.

 The United Bottle Project suggests an alternative use for PET
bottles, thousands of which are discarded each day. Drawing
on the stackable, refillable and easily shipped qualities of these
bottles, the prototypical idea by Instant Architects is to re-use
the vessels: first as water carriers and then as building materials. Once empty, the bottles
can be filled with soil or other materials available locally and stacked together to create
shelters in crisis situations or even to form temporary structures, such as repairs to
damaged buildings. This reconsidered approach to the way an everyday waste product
is typically recycled addresses the two main challenges in crisis zones: distributing safe
drinking water and constructing emergency shelter.

Project Name **Temporary Bar**		Location **Porto, Portugal**
Architect / Designer **LIKE Architects**		Date **2008**

Plastic tubs from IKEA might not seem like an immediate choice of building material, but 420 of them make up the knobbly skin of this pop-up bar. Designed by architectural students, Diogo Aguiar and Teresa Otto, for an annual competition held by the Oporto Architecture School, the bar is constructed from a steel-framed rectilinear volume standing 4.7 metres (15½ ft) tall, which is clad with modular wooden frames onto which the tubs are affixed. A folding hatch reveals the bar counter, and the entire structure is lit by LEDs at night, which pulse and change colour in response to the accompanying DJ set.

Project Name **Switch+**	Location **Münster, Germany**
Architect / Designer **Modulorbeat**	Date **2007**

 Designed to act as an 'urban switch' that could channel the flow of pedestrians by opening or closing part of its sliding facade, this temporary public space was part of Skulptur Projekte Münster 2007 and housed services for the exhibition inside its perforated skin. Enlivening what is normally an overlooked corner, the 12 metre (39½ ft) high gold-coloured casing of punched copper panels included space for an information point, tour guide rentals, catalogue sales and a specialty bookshop. Mounted on a simple steel frame, the radiant facades of Switch+ also provided shelter and overspill seating for the adjacent Skulptur Projekte café.

| Project Name **Sandworm** | Location **Wenduine, Belgium** |
| Architect / Designer **Marco Casagrande** | Date **2012** |

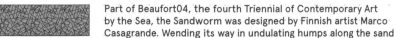 Part of Beaufort04, the fourth Triennial of Contemporary Art by the Sea, the Sandworm was designed by Finnish artist Marco Casagrande. Wending its way in undulating humps along the sand dunes of Wenduine beach, this 45 metre (147½ ft) long structure of woven willow is 10 metres (32¾ ft) wide and creates a space in which the public can relax, picnic or simply observe the natural spectacle of light and shadow within. The installation took four weeks to install and is constructed from large hoops of willow, secured to the sand at regular intervals. Like a gigantic basket, the willowy lengths were woven longitudinally between the supportive arches to form the body.

 Suspended from the ceiling in the narrow stairwell at Austria's OK Center for Contemporary Art in Linz, this steep black net staircase provided a temporary alternative for visitors to ascend and descend between levels of the gallery, sandwiched between a concrete wall and a staircase. Composed of two pairs of net mesh layers, weighed down by sandbags and articulated by steel rods, each of the layers encloses a traversable net ramp. Portholes that pierce the undulating net surfaces lead between the two stairways and allow visitors to choose their own path to the top. The net is designed to sway and move in response to the different weights of visitors and the paths they choose to ascend.

| Project Name **Sinestesia** | Location **Madrid, Spain** | Date **2013** |
| Architect / Designer **Plastique Fantastique with IED Madrid** | | |

 These leggy, elongated bubbles called Sinestesia are the result of a week-long workshop at Madrid's IED design school, led by Marco Canevacci of the architecture collective, Plastique Fantastique. Installed in the courtyard of IED and spilling from the building's upper windows into the street, the inflatable translucent tubes were designed and fabricated by fifteen students. The intervention is intended to question how private and public spaces are used – especially when occupied by such ephemeral building materials. Exposed visually, guests could isolate themselves spatially in the aerated tubes and experience the interactions of surprised passers-by who were taken aback by the effect of floating bubbles on the normal streetscape.

 The third tea house designed by A1 Architects, Hat is a 1.8 square metre (6 sq ft) oak structure clad in larch with an exaggerated shingle roof, which gives the project its name. Designed to accommodate three people for a quiet tea ceremony or for time to reflect on the surrounding gardens, the house has sliding screens that can be used to alter views out, and portions of the walls that can be winched open to form veranda roofs. Due to its small dimensions, the hearth for tea preparations is hidden inside a drawer in the larch bench. The broad seating is enclosed by a curved oak plywood wall, and crowned by hundreds of oak ribs that reach towards the circular skylight.

| Project Name **Swamp Hut** | Location **Massachussetts, USA** |
| Architect / Designer **Moskow Linn Architects** | Date **2008** |

Providing a simple retreat for two architects' families, the Swamp Hut is a collection of four small cabins arranged in a cross-shaped formation around a central square deck. Each cabin is an identical structure of 3.6 metre (11¾ ft) high timber trusses, which were prefabricated off-site and then installed, clad with aluminium and fibreglass panels. The tall gabled roofs create airy light-filled places to rest and socialize in summer; in winter the snow slips off the steep pitch. Containing 54 square metres (177 sq ft) of space for sleeping, dining and bathing, the huts offer the most basic amenities for the owners, who chose to keep the project off-grid, without electricity or running water.

| Project Name **CC4441** | | Location **Tokyo, Japan** | |
| Architect / Designer **Tomokazu Hayakawa Architects** | | Date **2014** | |

 Housing a small gallery at ground level and an office above, this 36 square metre (118 sq ft) project re-appropriates two shipping containers, stacking them across a tiny corner site in old downtown Tokyo. In order to meet Japanese building requirements, the architects turned the building functions inside out: the ramshackle sturdy containers are here rendered black and treated as skins while internal timber framing and steel bracing provides seismic and structural stability. The container doors are similarly reversed from their original function and open from the inside out, creating an engaging relationship between the exposed private spaces and the adjacent public footpath.

| Project Name **Walking House** | Location **Copenhagen, Denmark (or elsewhere)** |
| Architect / Designer **N55** | Date **2008** |

 Developed by Danish art collective, N55, The Walking House is an ecologically minded home, influenced by the travelling patterns of Romani wagons. Unlike its horse-drawn precedent, this self-sufficient 'wagon' can travel on its own six legs anywhere with the gait of an average human. Standing 3.5 metres (11½ ft) tall and wide, the polygonal house harvests energy from its surroundings as it walks via integrated solar panels and windmills. Equipped with modest areas for cooking, sleeping, bathing and living, the home is heated by an internal wood-burning stove and includes a composting toilet and rainwater collection. Built of a framework of steel, aluminium or wood, and clad with the same materials or with waterproof textiles, the house is accessed through operable polycarbonate windows.

Project Name **Inversion**	Location **Texas, USA**
Architect / Designer **Havel Ruck Projects**	Date **2007**

When the Art League Houston was faced with the demolition of two of its 1920s bungalows, they decided instead to commission sculptors Dan Havel and Dean Ruck of Havel Ruck Projects to work with the condemned structures and create a temporary installation. The result is *Inversion* and sits in contrast to the gabled homes adjacent to it. Subverting the usual order of such domestic materials, the explosive facade is an arresting visual surprise. Taking the reclaimed timber materials as a starting point, the artists stripped off the exterior weatherboard skins and used the splinters of wooden board to shore up a tunnel. Piercing through the central hallway of the houses, the large timber vortex runs all the way from the main facade through to a child-sized hole in the rear courtyard wall.

| Project Name **Recycled Pallet Pavilion** | Location **Florence, Italy** |
| Architect / Designer **Avatar Architettura** | Date **2010** |

This demountable pavilion was designed by Avatar Architettura for the garden of the Villa Romana – the German Cultural Institute in Florence. Formed of dozens of precast diamond-shaped wooden pallets, the pavilion created a self-supporting multifunctional space that housed exhibitions, performances, installations and other gatherings. Connected by custom-made metal joints, the recycled pallets were assembled in just four days and its design allowed for simple disassembly when no longer needed. An opaque and transparent PVC membrane protected guests inside the open-shell structure from rain and wind while still allowing views to the idyllic surroundings.

| Project Name | **Permanent Camping** | Location | **New South Wales, Australia** |
| Architect / Designer | **Casey Brown Architecture** | Date | **2007** |

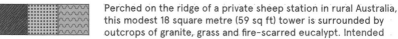 Perched on the ridge of a private sheep station in rural Australia, this modest 18 square metre (59 sq ft) tower is surrounded by outcrops of granite, grass and fire-scarred eucalypt. Intended as a retreat for the client, the 3 × 3 metre (9¾ × 9¾ ft) wide corrugated iron project is arranged over two storeys. The lower level is enclosed by glass louvres and full-height doors and contains the living space with a wood-fired stove. The upper level is accessed via ladder through a trapdoor that leads to the sleeping space, timber-clad. Corrugated iron cladding to the north, east and west facades can be winched open to create veranda roofs that protect against strong sunlight. On departure, the roofs are simply retracted to enclose the small cabin and protect it from weather and bush fires.

Project Name **Grooming Retreat**	Location **Mallorca, Spain**	Date **2014**
Architect / Designer **Gartnerfuglen Arkitekter with Mariana de Delás**		

 Rising up from the middle of a private barley field on the southern Spanish island of Mallorca, this Grooming Retreat is formed of three timber structures: an elevated platform for the rider, a feeding and grooming station for her horse, and a slim path that connects the two structures. Intended as a delicate retreat for solace and personal grooming, before and after riding and grooming the horse, the wooden tower is shielded by layers of mosquito netting that have increasing opacities, which correspond to the various of activities held within. Accessed via a ladder through a trapdoor in the floor, the platform is divided into spaces for the rider to cleanse mind, body and spirit, while also giving far-reaching views to the sea and coastal olive trees.

The ultimate example of transportable architecture, this small home of only 27 square metres (88½ sq ft) was designed specifically to be hoisted onto the bed of a truck and craned into a chosen location. Constructed of grey cement-board panels, Casa Transportable is organized around a central living room and kitchen, which is flanked by a bedroom and bathroom at each end. The panels hinge open to the front and ends of the elongated gabled house to reveal a glazed entry and allow light through the two small windows. The modest proportions of the house mean it can be manufactured in up to six weeks, and assembled in a single day.

In contrast to its inner-suburban neighbours, many of which are from the Victorian era, this contemporary two-bedroom house offers a friendly greeting to all that pass by. Designed by OOF! Architecture in collaboration with artist Rose Nolan, the white-brick wall spells out the word 'HELLO' at full height along its main facade. This gives the project a boldly cheerful face to the street while providing domestic privacy to its inhabitants. Only a narrow vertical window that pierces the 'O' offers a glimpse of the home and creative studio inside, which is a simple pavilion for work and rest.

Project Name **The Vigil**		Location **Saint-Mitre-les-Remparts, France**
Architect / Designer **OH!SOM Architectes**		Date **2014**

 Replacing temporary accommodation in the Figuerolles Park, near Martigues in France, this permanent one-legged watchtower stands on a natural promontory and is used as an elevated point from which to guard the surrounding forest during summer. To minimize both its building footprint and disturbance to the natural ecology of the site, the project was designed as a prefabricated, preassembled modular system clad in timber with a steel structural support and open terrace. The unobtrusive wooden cabin blends with its environment and provides 16 square metres (52½ sq ft) of shelter. All window openings can be fully covered by timber shutters, which act as brise-soleil when raised and secure the building when closed at the end of each summer.

Project Name **Buijtenbed**	Location **The Netherlands (or elsewhere)**
Architect / Designer **Studio Makkink and Bey**	Date **2012**

 Part of a cooperative project by Werkplaats Buijtenland that seeks to revive a Dutch agricultural polderland with recreational programs, the Buijtenbed is one of five mobile projects commissioned for the area. The mobile dwelling is essentially a caravan enclosed in a timber stall, which can be transported on the flat bed of a standard trailer to any desired location. The stall serves as a protective, moveable and mostly transparent case for the caravan, whose body has been partially removed to flood its interior with daylight. Like a caravan, the Buijtenbed is entirely self-contained and includes areas for sleeping, sitting and cooking, which are accessed from wide steps that also serve as a deck.

 One of several pavilions designed for the Jinhua Architecture Park, each selected by Chinese artist Ai Weiwei, the Jinhua Structure I-Cube by Herzog & De Meuron is imagined as a kind of 'virtual library' for the park. Built from dyed concrete using conventional construction methods, the irregular form of the pavilion derives from the idea of intersecting lines of an imaginary spatial grid that were either solidified or scooped out to create a three-dimensional geometric pattern. The result is one of three pavilions designed using this method: in this case creating an unusual yet useable series of spaces such as benches, platforms, roofs, caves and tree houses that can be climbed over or sat on by adults and children alike.

| Project Name **10 Cal Tower** | Location **Chonburi, Thailand** |
| Architect / Designer **Supermachine Studio** | Date **2014** |

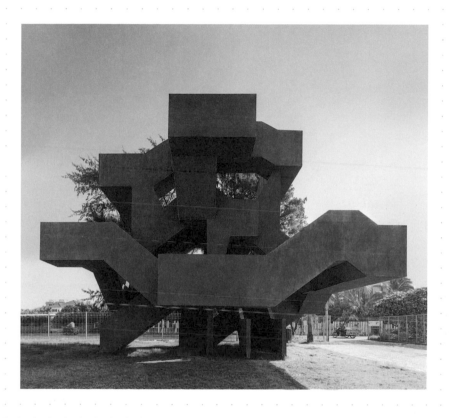

 Constructed of hefty rust-coloured concrete, this playground is known as 10 Cal Tower and was one of three public structures built to celebrate the centenary of Thailand's largest construction company, Siam Cement Group. Motivated to design a place where parents and their children could interact, the playground does away with normal play equipment and is instead a kind of elevated labyrinth. Like an Escher drawing, there are dozens of different pathways to race up, hide in, rest on or to use as a viewing platform to observe activities in the adjacent public park and along the coast. The tower's moniker derives from the calorific value burned when walking from top to bottom at normal speed.

| Project Name **The Warp** | Location **Shuanghe, Yunnan Province, China** |
| Architect / Designer **John Lin and Olivier Ottevaere** | Date **2015** |

The final in a series of three timber projects designed and built in China's Yunnan Province by Olivier Ottevaere and John Lin with Hong Kong University students, The Warp straddles the edge of a steep valley and provides a rest area and roadside market for the Ludian township. Its humped form creates three zones for locals, including a stepped area for selling wares, a wooden deck for far-reaching scenic views, and a sheltered resting and eating area tucked below. The sinuous deck mimics the shape of the landscape and creates an arresting form while costing very little to build. As with the two preceding projects, The Warp is part of an effort to revitalize the earthquake-ravaged town by exploring low-cost timber constructions.

| Project Name **Jeffry's House** | Location **County Donegal, Republic of Ireland** |
| Architect / Designer **Emily Mannion and Thomas O'Brien** | Date **2014** |

This shaggy timber pavilion perches on a cliff edge in the Ards Forest Park in Ireland – the result of a collaboration between artist Emily Mannion and architect Thomas O'Brien. Winning a competition set by the Irish Architecture Foundation for a structure that would enhance its natural surroundings, the humped viewing platform of larch and flax thatch is a playful place to hide in, climb on, or simply take in the vista of distant sea and sand dunes. Openings at both short ends frame views through the lookout while roof lights permit rain and sunlight to enter. The unusual textured structure attracts visitors from the local playground to discover what's inside.

Representing the UK at Shanghai's 2010 Expo, the Seed Pavilion was intended to convey the country's connection between cities and nature in a way that would also be popular with the public. Standing 20 metres (65½ ft) tall and pierced by more than 60,000 fibre-optic rods, the pavilion is a light conductor: each of the 7.5 metre (24½ ft) long translucent rods pass through the steel and timber structure, drawing daylight into the 'seed chamber'. Embedded with a light source, at night the rods direct light outward to create a glowing 'hairy' haze. The tip of each rod is embedded with plant seeds – more than 217,300 in total – that were collected in association with Kew Gardens' Millennium Seedbank.

Tubakuba is the result of a collaborative design-and-build workshop between Bergen School of Architecture students and architect Espen Folgerø, to create an 'urban cottage' that was accessible from the city yet situated within a forest. Perched on the edge of a rocky outcrop, visitors enter the distinctive 14 square metre (46 sq ft) retreat through a child-sized vortex created from layers of steamed, western Norwegian pine that have been bent into the shape of a tuba. The conical entry is framed by charred pine walls prepared with the traditional Japanese method *shou sugi ban* that gives resilllence against decay and damage. The textured exterior gives way to a plywood interior with a large picture window that frames views across the city.

| Project Name **Story Tower** | Location **Cēsis, Latvia** |
| Architect / Designer **Riga Technical Universityt** | Date **2013** |

 This semi-permanent library by students at Riga Technical University stands in the centre of Cēsis and creates a quiet, sheltered area for the public to freely browse and exchange books. Conceived as a large urban lamp, the miniature, illuminated library is stocked with deaccessioned books donated by the local library and from members of the public. The polygonal structure is clad with 2,250 unfolded Tetra Pak cartons handmade from a 100 kilogram (220 lb) roll and fixed to the timber frame, forming a silvery, shingled skin that is both reflective and waterproof. Lined with timber bookshelves, the folly is illuminated by daylight flooding through the tower's crown.

Project Name **M-velopes**		Location **USA (or elsewhere)**
Architect / Designer **Michael Jantzen**		Date **2014**

Reminiscent of an elaborate, expanded Cape Cod deck chair, the M-velope series by Michael Jantzen are private art retreats that differ from usual studio accommodation. Each piece evolves from a simpler form, which is then subdivided, hinged and folded to create a complex series of shapes of different scales that can be mounted together to form a larger workspace. Deliberately designed for easy transportation, the M-velopes are composed of slotted timber panels, a support frame, floor, and ramps, all of which can be demounted for shipping and reassembled.

Project Name **The Youth Wing for Art Education Entrance Courtyard**	Date **2014**
Architect / Designer **Ifat Finkelman and Deborah Warschawski**	Location **Jerusalem, Israel**

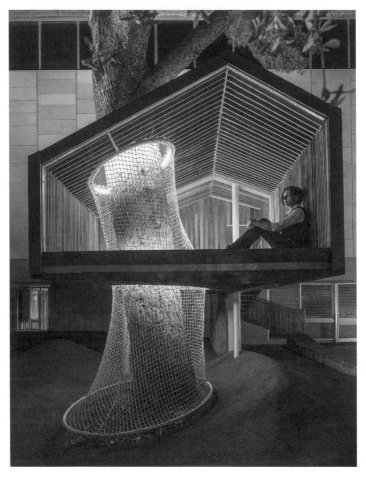

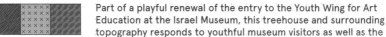 Part of a playful renewal of the entry to the Youth Wing for Art Education at the Israel Museum, this treehouse and surrounding topography responds to youthful museum visitors as well as the courtyard's established pine tree. The main focus is the elevated cabin, which encircles the lofty pine and is framed by a light steel skeleton wrapped by slats of 20 millimetre (¾ in) timber boards. The treehouse is flanked by a ramp, fireman's poles and durable mesh, which sheathes the trunk and creates a climbing surface for children. Below the play equipment, an undulating soft rubber surface invites visitors to run, play, or rest; at the same time it softens a tumble and provides protection for the broad tree roots.

| Project Name | **Mirrored Tree House** | Location | **Harads, Sweden** |
| Architect / Designer | **Tham and Videgård Arkitekter** | Date | **2010** |

 Part of the eco-tourist Tree Hotel complex in Sweden, the Mirrorcube is a mirrored glass box, just 4 cubic metres (39½ cu ft), that is built around a pine trunk and accessed by a 12 metre (13 ft) long rope bridge suspended from neighbouring trees. Reflecting the ethos of Tree Hotel, the cabin is a respite for two that is designed to blend in with the forest, wildlife and sky around it and give panoramic views across the remote landscape from the six windows and rooftop terrace. Framed in aluminium, the mirrored facade contrasts with the diminutive pale plywood interior, which accommodates a double bed, bathroom and lounge.

Project Name **Chairs for Abu Dhabi**	Location **Abu Dhabi, United Arab Emirates**
Architect / Designer **Tadashi Kawamata**	Date **2012**

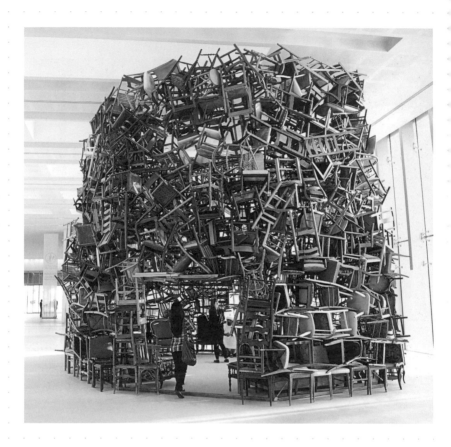

This large dome of stacked seating is consistent with the language of Tadashi Kawamata's oeuvre, which often uses repurposed or found objects as raw material to work with. *Chairs for Abu Dhabi* is a 6 metre (19¾ ft) high cupola of 1,000 stacked chairs that almost reach the gallery's ceiling and allowed people to pass through, meet at, or rest on the sculpture. The work included a diverse range of seating, including armchairs, sofas, benches and stools, all of which were amassed and assembled by twenty people over five days. The different timbers, upholstery and shapes of the chairs form a rich textural body towering in the space and acted as a visual beacon for the Abu Dhabi Biennale.

Project Name **Electrified Line**	Location **Folkestone, England, UK**
Artist / Designer **Gabriel Lester**	Date **2014**

In contrast to the weighty nineteenth-century brick railway arches on which it stands, Electrified Line is a lightweight temporary pavilion made of hundreds of pieces of bamboo atop a timber base, marking the end of the disused Folkestone Harbour Branch railway. Part of the 2014 Folkestone Triennale, the pavilion was designed by the Dutch-born, Chinese-based artist Gabriel Lester who was inspired by the building materials native to his new home. The spiky chorus of bamboo poles is arranged to enclose timber stairs that lead to an observation deck from which visitors can survey the track or the harbour and horizon

MACRO

Project Name **Tee Haus**		Location **Frankfurt am Main, Germany**
Architect / Designer **Kengo Kuma and Associates**		Date **2007**

Kengo Kuma and Associates' Tee Haus is a 31 square metre (101¾ sq ft) temporary venue for tea ceremonies that was installed in Frankfurt during the summer. In contrast to most tea houses, this version is made from a double-layered membrane of Tenara, a pliable material that can subtly expand and contract when inflated. The two membranes are connected by polyester string and joints at 600 millimetre (23½ in) intervals, which connect the inflatable layers and create a texture of points inside and out, like a quilted igloo. The semi-translucent skin allows the changing patterns of sunlight and cloud to filter through by day; at night the exterior glows from within.

Project Name **'Ban' Pavilion**	Location **Beijing, China**
Architect / Designer **Orproject**	Date **2012**

 This self-supporting pavilion built from bent polymer sheets was designed by Orproject for the 2012 Beijing Design Week and takes its inspiration from the way petals inform how a flower is shaped. Similarly, the technique for how polymer sheets bend can be predicted according to the material's known anisotropy in that it behaves differently in compression than in tension. This knowledge informed the basis of the multitude of single-curved 'petal' elements that shape the system of columns, arches and vaults in the pavilion. Following this logic, the polymer sheets are simply bolted at regular intervals to create a diaphanous billowing form, in contrast to the weighty historic *hutongs* nearby.

| Project Name **Small House** | Location **Hohenecken, Germany** |
| Architect / Designer **Architekturbüro Scheder** | Date **2015** |

 Severely restricted by local planning requirements and the proximity to neighbours, this minute house is just 12 metres (39½ ft) long and 3.5 metres (11½ ft) wide and sits above a grassy slope on the edge of a forest. From the street, the tiny facade is blankly clad with grey-painted Douglas fir and its box-like appearance on narrow stilts gives no clue to the house that stretches out behind it. The long, narrow house follows the incline of the hill in profile, and includes a shiny cylindrical podium at ground level containing amenities and storage; living, dining and kitchen spaces at raised ground level; and a bedroom and bathroom on the upper level, tucked beneath the half-pitched roof. Though small, the home is flooded with light from large picture windows that flank its sides.

Project Name **Bow-House**	Location **Heerlen, The Netherlands**
Architect / Designer **Stéphane Malka**	Date **2014**

Clinging to a graffitied brick wall in the Netherlands, this incongruent patchwork of reclaimed doors and windows is a nomadic domestic installation, accessible to all and replicable by anyone. The impermanent dwelling by architect Stéphane Malka is supported by a framework of scaffolding that parasitically borrows from the plaza's wall to create its fourth facade. The structure is arranged over three levels, including bedrooms, living spaces, an outdoor area for dining and a grassed terrace. Inspired by Nas' rap lyrics in 'The World is Yours', Malka responded with this cheap, readily available system that can add practical commodity to neglected urban sites.

Project Name **Upper Branch Tree House**	Location **Kaikoura, New Zealand**
Architect / Designer **Wilson Architects**	Date **2006**

Overlooking the surf beach of Mangamanu Bay and part of a deer farm on New Zealand's remote east coast, the Upper Branch Tree Houses are part of Hapuku Lodge, a contemporary country hotel designed by a family of architects and builders. Each Tree House stands 10 metres (32¾ ft) above the ground and hovers over the canopy of a native Manuka grove, giving views to Kaikoura's coastline and mountainous terrain. Clad in native timber and copper shingles, the interiors of the intimate retreats are almost entirely fitted with locally produced wooden furniture, and also include a wood-burning stove and a rain fountain shower that opens directly onto a private tree-top deck.

Project Name **GRID**	Location **Sydney, New South Wales, Australia (or elsewhere)**
Architect / Designer **Carter Williamson Architects**	Date **2012**

Prompted by the destruction of the Banda Aceh tsunami and in response to increasingly regular natural and man-made disasters, Carter Williamson Architects designed this emergency GRID housing. The insulated steel-framed structure is pre-fabricated and flat-packed, and can be assembled in as little as four hours. Based on standard units of materials and truck capacities, the housing can be transported by road to remote locations – its inverted Acrow prop feet act as support columns that can be adjusted for stability according to uneven terrain. Fitted with photovoltaic cells, rainwater tanks and a solar hot-water system, and with separate ablution and sanitary amenities, GRID is effectively a permanent home that can house up to ten people.

| Project Name | **Serpentine Pavilion 2002** | | Location | **London, England, UK** |
| Architect / Designer | **Toyo Ito** | | Date | **2002** |

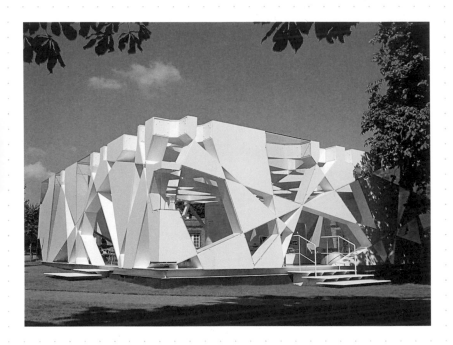

 In collaboration with engineer Cecil Balmond and ARUP, Toyo Ito was the third architect to be commissioned by the Serpentine Gallery for its annual summer pavilion. Though the complex triangles and trapezoids of the pavilion appear to be a random composition of steel and glass, the design was underpinned by a clear intention: to transform the most humble of architectural volumes – a box. Its simple cubic geometry was criss-crossed by a network of lines and crossings, which were then built as supportive steel blades painted white, intersected by a chequered pattern of inserted glass and aluminium panels.

Project Name **Curtain**	Location **New York, New York, USA**	
Architect / Designer **Jerome W. Haferd and K. Brandt Knapp**		Date **2012**

Curtain is the winning design for a folly installed temporarily in New York's Socrates Sculpture Park, Queens, organized in association with The Architectural League. The ephemeral geometric structure is a complex construction made of simple components - 100 × 100 millimetre (4 × 4 in) timber laths, steel joints and hundreds of metres of white plastic chain. Set within an orthogonal grid, the volume of the folly is formed by timber frames that rise and fall around the perimeter walls and span across the form to create a skeleton of intersecting, chamfered planes. Painted white, and draped with glossy white chain, the project provides a curtained place in which to play and the chain links form a dynamic, moving threshold between the park and the space inside.

MICRO

MINI

MIDI

MACRO

MAXI

| Project Name | **Hut on Sleds** | Location | **Coromandel Peninsula, New Zealand (or elsewhere)** |
| Architect / Designer | **Crosson Carnachan Clarke** | Date | **2012** |

Yielding to local requirements for all buildings on this coastal erosion zone to be removable, the Hut on Sleds is a holiday home for a family of five and is literally mounted on two solid timber sleds. This practical arrangement allows the 40 square metre (131¼ sq ft) hut to be towed further up the site, or across the beach to be transported elsewhere by barge. Rough macrocarpa timber planks envelop the home and are incised on the beach facade to form a huge shutter, which can be folded up to reveal the entry and provide shade for the enormous double-height glazed facade. This dramatic portico gives extensive views to the ocean from all rooms of the open-plan interior, as well as from the roof deck hidden behind the parapet.

| Project Name | **Mini House 2.0** | Location | **Sweden (or elsewhere)** |
| Architect / Designer | **Jonas Wagell** | Date | **2015** |

This 15 square metre (49¼ sq ft) house by Jonas Wagell was designed as a simple elegant timber shed for use as a guest house or a place to retreat to. Built from a prefabricated volume that is carefully scaled in size for optimized shipping, the Mini House 2.0 can be simply transferred to site with a mobile crane. Formed largely of timber for both structure and interior finishes, the houses can also be tailored to include facilities for cooking, bathing, sleeping and storage. Though the smaller model is standard, the basic unit can be combined to form a Long or Wide version: an elongated or broader house, up to 45 square metres (147½ sq ft)

| Project Name **House A** | Location **Vilches, Chile** |
| Architect / Designer **Smiljan Radić** | Date **2008** |

This A-shaped house by Smiljan Radić in Chile's VII Maule Region is described as a type of 'domestic cave' built around the existing environment, which included sixty large blocks of basalt scattered across the site – and through the house itself. Surrounded by forest, the house sits on a black dais that forms the ground floor and slopes down on either side like a low dark mound, easing the transition between inside and out. The building's close relationship to context is emphasized by the large doors, that can hinge open to fully expose the heart of the dwelling. Sheltered by an asphalt-coated membrane the apex of the house contains small bedrooms and an external observation deck from which to contemplate the distant hills.

Project Name **Charred Cabin**	Location **Santiago, Chile**
Architect / Designer **DRAA**	Date **2014**

Containing a place to eat, sleep, bathe and read, this humble black cabin in the Santiago mountains is an exercise in simplicity. Its 15 square metre (49¼ ft) footprint contains all the basic necessities for a retreat, including a small kitchen, bathroom and living area, with a sleeping platform above. Sitting atop timber pillars, the cabin was constructed from prefabricated structural insulated panels, which allowed for swift construction and minimal material costs. Its characteristic charred pine planks mimic a natural Japanese technique that protects the exterior from weather and insect damage. Inside, black detailing of the mezzanine ladder and timber columns continues the blackened theme and contrasts with the warm timber hue of the plywood interior.

This tower of timber batons was created by Belgian artist, Arne Quinze, one of many site-specific installations at the Burning Man festival in Nevada's Black Rock Desert. The work forms part of his continuing intention to broaden people's horizons through art. It required 150 kilometres (93 mi) of wooden laths, which were cut to different lengths and nailed into place over a three-week period. Once assembled, Uchronia stood 15 metres (49¼ ft) high and created a meeting place that was patterned with stippled light by day; by night the structure was brightly lit and cast irregular shadows across the sand. Though striking, the sculpture's presence was short-lived: engulfed by flames, its dramatic finale was as an enormous bonfire – an appropriate conclusion for the scorching festival.

Project Name	ICD/ITKE Research Pavilion	Location	Stuttgart, Germany
Architect / Designer	University of Stuttgart ICD and ITKE	Date	2011

The Institute for Computational Design (ICD) and the Institute of Building Structures and Structural Design (ITKE) collaborated on the design and construction of this experimental folly, which brings together the structure of a sand dollar (Echinoidea) with the computational tools of architecture and design. Built from 275 square metres (902¼ sq ft) of birch plywood sheets only 6.5 millimetres (¼ in) thick, the natural efficiency and strength of the sand dollar's plate is writ large in the resulting arched timber form, which extends 72 square metres (236¼ sq ft). The structure is made from differently sized polygonal components that connect via a series of finger joints. Fabricated robotically, each plywood cell is joined with screws so that the folly can be assembled and disassembled with ease.

Project Name **Vieux Port Pavilion**	Location **Marseille, France**
Architect / Designer **Foster + Partners**	Date **2013**

Once a historically significant maritime entrance to France, Marseille's Vieux Port had been in decline for decades but this reflective pavilion is one part of extensive regeneration of the city's World Heritage-listed harbour. Supported by eight slender pillars, the razor-thin canopy of mirror-finished stainless steel appears to float, providing shelter from sun and rain, and creating a focal point in the open square for concerts, markets and civic celebrations. From afar, the pavilion appears to be a silver line on the horizon while up close the lightweight 46 × 22 metre (151 × 72 ft) structure reflects sunlight, activities in the harbour and the life of the Marseillais.

| Project Name | **Concert Hall** | | Location | **Gauja, Latvia** |
| Architect / Designer | **Didzis Jaunzems Architecture** | | Date | **2014** |

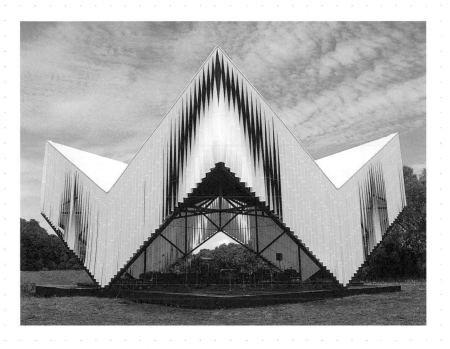

Creating a fitting frame for the environmentally themed event 'Nature's Concert Hall', and sited in a designated biotope meadow, this concert hall by Didzis Jaunzems Architecture is designed to touch the earth lightly while providing shelter and necessary acoustic insulation. The zig-zagging steel frame rests on just four points and is clad with bands of acoustic textile, which can be rotated like louvres. When open they allow music to travel further afield while filtering light in; when closed they create a taut screen for scenographic projections. A simple platform for a symphonic chamber orchestra of twenty musicians forms the base.

This range of prototypical housing was designed to be constructed in the Western Ghats – a 1600 kilometre (994 mi) long mountain range in India that is internationally recognized as a notable area for biodiversity. Drawing on local building techniques, the simple huts are intended to encourage eco-tourism in the Ghats. By selecting construction techniques and materials that maximise environmental responsibility, such as locally available timber and bamboo, the designs inspire simplicity of production and ease of long-term maintenance. All huts run off-grid from solar roof panels and can stand alone, or be clustered together to form a shaded courtyard in between the houses.

| Project Name **House in Horinouchi** | Location **Tokyo, Japan** |
| Architect / Designer **Kota Mizuishi** | Date **2011** |

Hemmed in by a river and an access road, this two-storey home by Kota Mizuishi makes the most of the tight restrictions of its tiny triangular site. Its steel-clad upper floor cantilevers beyond the ground level perimeter, providing views to the river, a sheltered car park and allowing for 55.24 square metres (181¼ sq ft) of space to house a family of three. From the ground floor, which contains the master bedroom and bathroom, the inhabitants ascend to the first-floor living spaces and kitchen that are open plan and orientate towards the river-facing balcony. A second bedroom at this level is fitted with a ladder that leads to the airy mezzanine loft, which sits beneath the hipped steel roof and is punctuated by rooflights.

| Project Name **Parkside Pavilion** | Location **London, England, UK** |
| Architect / Designer **DSDHA** | Date **2007** |

In contrast to the stark glass and steel buildings of City Hall that tower above it, this charred pavilion with its oversized timber cantilever creates a small sheltered public space for park and café patrons. The architects were inspired by the history of the site, which was severely bombed during World War II, so the pavilion is formed of stacked, burned timber and houses a café, public conveniences and storage. Drawing on the traditional Japanese technique of *shou sugi ban* to burn and preserve timber, the Parkside Pavilion was designed as one of a pair at Potters' Fields Park beside London's iconic Tower Bridge. It is imagined as an urban grotto in the context of England's historic romantic landscapes.

Project Name **Spacebuster**	Location **New York, New York, USA (or elsewhere)**
Architect / Designer **Raumlabor**	Date **2009**

This collaboration between Raumlabor and the Storefront for Art and Architecture exploits the idea of a truck-borne public space, housing a nomadic place for the public to gather within a gigantic translucent plastic bubble. Called Spacebuster, the enormous bubble is housed in the back of a small truck, which holds the equipment to aerate the inflated transparent space, hosting a variety of public events. Entirely moveable, the minimal domed form can accommodate up to eighty people and the parties, concerts, dinners, films or discussions that occur inside are totally visible from outside. Conversely, the environment that Spacebuster occupies becomes its backdrop.

Project Name **Lake Cabin**	Location **Doksy, Czech Republic**
Architect / Designer **FAM Architekti**	Date **2014**

 Respecting the same boundaries as its predecessor – a 1970s cabin with poor insulation and infrastructure – this wedge-shaped cabin provides a retreat for a yachting enthusiast. Standing on large steel screws amid a pine forest, its slatted timber facade wraps the retreat and forms a folding timber screen; when closed, its shutters protect the full-width window that faces the lake. In good weather, the entire south-west facade can be retracted and opened to the lakeside, providing a truly indoor-outdoor living space.
Inside, all of the main surfaces are clad in pale oiled timber battens, continuing the connection between forest and cabin. The wedge-shaped form allows for a shallow mezzanine sleeping platform to fit above a modest kitchen and bathroom.

| Project Name **Tea House** | Location **Prague, Czech Republic** |
| Architect / Designer **A1 Architects** | Date **2008** |

Situated in a small garden between the Hloubetin and Aloisov hills, this teahouse is designed as an inconspicuous place for friends to gather for tea ceremonies, meditation and companionship. Built on a circular platform of oak, enclosed by burned larch slats, and elevated by stones recovered from a nearby pond, the sphere-shaped house references traditional Japanese *shoji* screens with its sliding paper and timbered walls. Inside, the focus is on a hearth of welded black steel, which is used to prepare water for making tea. Here the Japanese theme continues with flooring of reed mats. Built by the architect and builder in thirty-five days, the 7 square metre (23 sq ft) house is a modest addition to the garden that is intended to express the quietude and solace found within it.

| Project Name **Coca-Cola Beatbox** | Location **London, England, UK** |
| Architect / Designer **Asif Khan and Pernilla Ohrstedt** | Date **2012** |

Part of the London 2012 Olympic Games, this interactive Beatbox sponsored by Coca-Cola was a fusion of architecture, music, sport and technology, intended to popularize the Games for young people. Like a human-scale mixing deck, Beatbox was composed of 200 interlocking red and white ETFE plastic pillows – each the size of a billboard – which were sensitive to movement and touch. As visitors ascended the pavilion's ramp, certain pillows could be 'played' to emit recorded sound samples: from athlete's heartbeats to squeaking running shoes and samples from the Olympic song 'Anywhere in the World'. Its striking red and white crystalline structure references the sponsor's iconic colours and acted as a beacon in the expansive Olympic Park arena.

Project Name **Kubik**	Location **Vevey, Switzerland (or elsewhere)**
Architect / Designer **Balestra Berlin**	Date **2013**

This mobile installation by German-based collective, Balestra Berlin, was originally created to capitalize on abandoned urban spaces for club nights, using simple water tanks as a basic building block. The cubic water tanks are secured to form stacking walls, suspended ceilings, and can even be used to house events that float on water. Each is illuminated by specialized lighting techniques that allow the cubes to glow with a spectrum of vibrant colours, and in an array of intensities and patterns. Since launching in 2006, the Kubik club has been installed many times around Europe and can expand or contract in size to accommodate a range of audiences – from an intimate gathering for 200, to a mass party for 8,000.

Project Name **Tower Studio**	Location **Fogo Island, Newfoundland, Canada**
Architect / Designer **Saunders Architecture**	Date **2011**

One of several arts studios commissioned by the Fogo Island Arts Corporation, this kinked tower is sited in the remote Shoal Bay and is accessible only by foot. From afar, the abstract silhouette appears to be cloaked with a windowless skin of black-painted spruce boards and gives no clue as to its function. Its crooked shape results from a floor plan that is rotated 180 degrees, and it is only on approach that a clue to the entrance niche is given by white stained spruce boards lining the recessed portico. The 10 metre (32¾ ft) tall studio is arranged over three levels and houses a kitchenette, bathroom and wood-burning fireplace at ground level, a studio at first floor, and a mezzanine platform above, which leads to the roof deck.

| Project Name **Reading Between the Lines** | Location **Borgloon, Belgium** |
| Architect / Designer **Pieterjan Gijs and Arnout Van Vaerenbergh** | Date **2011** |

 Part of a public art initiative Z-OUT by Z33 Gallery, *Reading Between the Lines* is located in the rural Belgian landscape of Borgloon and was based on the form of local churches nearby, many of which are vacant or under-used. Using a series of 100 stacked weathered steel plates, the architects re-composed the typical ecclesiastic shapes of a nave and steeple into a see-through church. Each plate hovers above the other to create gaps in the 10 metre (32¾ ft) high sculpture, which appears as a dense metallic form from one viewpoint, or a rusted floating spectre from another. From inside the church, views out to the landscape are framed by steel partitions.

Project Name **L'Observatoire**	Location **Muttersholtz, France**
Architect / Designer **Atelier 565**	Date **2012**

Concealed by a forest in a protected natural area of the Alsace region, this three-storey timber tower was built by Atelier 565 for the Archi<20 competition. Their intention was to make a building with the minimum amount of materials but that would offer maximum opportunities to engage with the building itself and its surroundings. The 20 square metre (65½ sq ft) interior is formed of three open-plan floors, each linked by a ladder, that were imagined as stages of a theatre to be reimagined anew with each visitor. The tower is enclosed by a wooden grid of walls, clad with panels of timber, glass or mirror, creating a disparate exterior pattern akin to a dislocated chequerboard.

Enchanted by the myth of the sea serpent in the neighbouring lake, the municipality of Seljord commissioned Rintala Eggertsson Architects to create lookout points for visitors and locals to enjoy the natural scenery and wildlife nearby. This five-storey-high wooden tower forms one part of the commission and is a striking marker for the small town, sited between two large pine trees and the lake. Its staircase winds to the top, past large picture windows that frame a bird nesting area and the crowns of the large pine trees. Once visitors reach the top, a full-width window gives far-reaching views across the fabled lake and to the landscape beyond. By day its slatted timber shell blends with the forested environment and by night it becomes a beacon on the edge of the lake.

| Project Name **Khor I** | Location **Venlo, The Netherlands** | Date **2012** |

| Architect / Designer **TAAT (Theatre as Architecture, Architecture as Theatre)** |

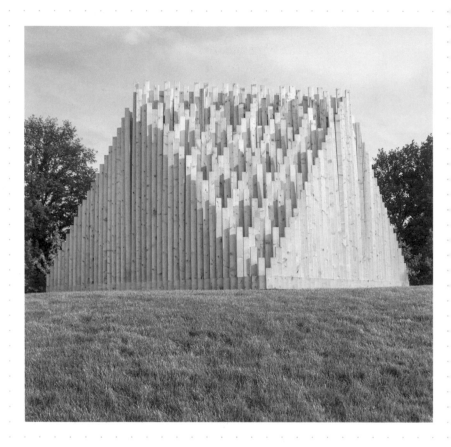

Designed for the 2012 World Horticultural Festival at Venlo, the concept for this interactive wooden pavilion for theatre was inspired by a walk through a bamboo forest where the vertical culms of bamboo create a defined area that is also visually open. The experience of Khor I mimics this, creating intimacy and accessibility at the same time. Constructed from hundreds of timber batons with identical dimensions slotting into a timber base, the pavilion has four sloping edges, each with a textured pyramidal shape. Visitors enter through a narrow break in the patterned facade to reach a smaller cubic space, which is also defined by the batons and serves as a small theatre.

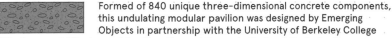
Formed of 840 unique three-dimensional concrete components, this undulating modular pavilion was designed by Emerging Objects in partnership with the University of Berkeley College of Environmental Design and the Siam Cement Group in Thailand. Exploring the new possibilities of printing buildings, each rectilinear block is powder-printed from Portland cement and carries a 'pixel' of the overall Thai blossom pattern – the motif becomes clear once the components are assembled. Arranged in a sinuous cruciform pattern and standing almost 3 metres (9¾ ft) tall, the diaphanous form is held in place using steel hardware and includes an entrance aperture incized into the angled walls.

| Project Name **The Sweep** | Location **Shuanghe, Yunnan Province, China** |
| Architect / Designer **John Lin and Olivier Ottevaere** | Date **2014** |

One of three experimental pavilions instigated by Professors Olivier Ottevaere and John Lin at the University of Hong Kong, The Sweep was constructed by sixty-five architecture students in just six days. The project acts as a meeting point, play area and viewing point to the mountains and rice fields in the village of Tuanjie, Yunnan Province. Rather than creating one fixed place to stand, Ottevaere and Lin conceived of a platform that encourages people to walk around the viewing area, to survey the landscape from different standpoints. Built from a series of twelve connected tangential trusses, the result is a rigid oval platform that cantilevers over the cliff top, punctuated by a central open ellipse, which creates an exposed courtyard in the undercroft.

Project Name **Timmelsjoch Experience Pass Museum**	Location **South Tyrol, Italy**
Architect / Designer **Werner Tscholl**	Date **2010**

Built to celebrate the fiftieth anniversary of the Timmelsjoch High Alpine Road, this small museum cantilevers precariously above the pass on the cusp between the north and south Tyrolean borders. Its chamfered steel carapace protrudes 16 metres (52¼ ft) into South Tyrol and is inspired by the rocks and boulders that characterize the region, mimicking the natural topography and hazardous conditions braved by those who constructed the pass. Inside, full-height faceted glass lines the walls and seals the two open ends of the steel frame. Recalling an ice cave, the glazing is inscribed with historic photographs that describe the arduous construction of the 12 kilometre (39½ mi) long pass.

Project Name **Diamond Island Community Hall**	Location **Ho Chi Minh City, Vietnam**
Architect / Designer **Vo Trong Nghia Architects**	Date **2014**

Providing flexible spaces for local residents, these domes by Vo Trong Nghia span 24 metres (78¾ ft) and are formed from a woven lattice of bamboo, a building material the architect calls, 'the green steel of the twenty-first century'. Rooted into a concrete base, the design of the eight domes is founded on the traditional Vietnamese basket weaving technique to carry birds. Here, they are over-scaled to create a place that accommodates conferences, meetings, children's activities, banquets and a restaurant. In contrast to the high-rise condominiums nearby, the community facilities are light, open and efficiently built from the abundant local supply of bamboo.

Project Name **ICD/ITKE Research Pavilion**	Location **Stuttgart, Germany**
Architect / Designer **University of Stuttgart ICD and ITKE**	Date **2010**

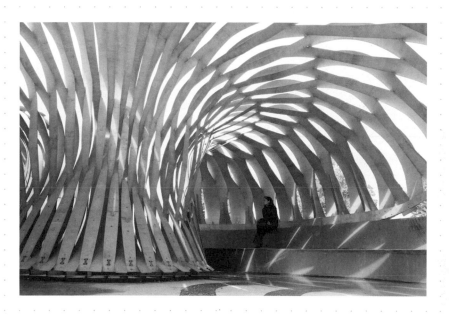

The result of research by Stuttgart University's Institute of Computational Design (ICD) and the Institute of Building Structures and Structural Design (ITKE), this experimental plywood pavilion is unusual in that it was designed using computational design tools but responds to the very tangible physical qualities of the birch plywood components. More than 500 geometrically unique parts constitute the pavilion, each of which was robotically manufactured as a planar element and then bolted and tensioned to form the interlocking curvaceous shape. The lightweight canopy is especially sensitive to wind and snow loading, and the design allows for this in its organization of components and by using plywood sheets only 6.5 millimetres (¼ in) deep, which minimizes the structural load.

| Project Name **Silent City** | Location **Rotterdam, the Netherlands (or elsewhere)** |
| Artist / Designer **Rob Sweere** | Date **2014** |

 This collection of three gigantic inflatable 'rooms' by Rob Sweere was commissioned by Art Rotterdam for the 2014 International Art Fair and is imagined as a group of inhabitable soft white islands that offer peace and tranquillity in the face of a busy metropolis. Visitors to the installation are invited to remove their shoes and lie in the stretched white vinyl skin of the large circular space, which is inflated with air and secured by guy ropes. In contrast to the relentless barrage of media, people and noise in most cities, the interior experience of Silent City is calmly devoid of such distractions.

Project Name **Light Cave**	Location **New York, New York, USA**
Architect / Designer **FriendsWithYou**	Date **2014**

 This radiant, multi-coloured elephantine structure by FriendsWithYou was commissioned by the Art Production Fund and The Standard Hotel and spanned the full length of the hotel's plaza for a month. Standing 7.5 metres (24½ ft) high, the Light Cave was imagined as a fully immersive experience for guests to pass through into the hotel and for visitors on the High Line, New York's elevated linear park, to wonder at. The skin of the temporary inflatable folly is coloured with rainbow hues that brighten the grey urban context by day. At night, the amorphous body is lit from within to create a glowing spectacle that floods the entrance and café tables nearby with colour.

Stretching out like tentacles of a creature from the deep, the Shellstar Pavilion was commissioned for the art and design festival, Detour, and provided a diverting meeting point over the course of the event. Formed of 4 millimetre (¼ in) translucent Coroplast cells, bound by cable ties to PVC and steel arches, the 8 × 8 metre (26¼ × 26¼ ft) pavilion rises and falls according to self-organizing catenary surfaces. Each of the almost 1,500 cells was unique and designed with advanced computational methods, which maximize the spatial arrangement of the piece but with a minimum of material and weight.

Project Name **EKKO**	Location **Hjallerup, Denmark**
Architect / Designer **Thilo Frank**	Date **2012**

Twisting around a circular concrete path in the middle of a meadow, this permanent public installation is formed by a tunnel of 200 wooden frames that form a contorted loop of timber with inbuilt microphones to record and play back the noise of visitor's footfall passing within it. Each of the 3 metre (9¾ ft) tall frames is set apart slightly from the next and falls at a marginally distorted angle, which creates a sense of torsion as guests pass through the circle. The gaps between frames add further visual warp when the sun passes overhead and casts elongated shadow stripes across the 20 metre (65½ ft) wide space. Seen from afar, the moiré of timber lattice hints at the sculpture's perceptual qualities.

| Project Name **Shelter No.2** | Location **Naucalpan, Mexico (or elsewhere)** |
| Architect / Designer **Broisson Architects** | Date **2008** |

Arranged around a central spiral staircase, this three-storey house responds to growing interest in small, prefabricated homes that can be constructed with relative ease and economy. The snug home for three includes a kitchen, bathroom, study, living areas and bedrooms, as well as a hydroponic garden at ground level. Arranged around the lozenge-shaped structural steel frame, Shelter No.2 is enclosed by a modular façade that dovetails together and is made almost entirely of recycled materials. Hexagonal openings puncture the pale steel sheets to admit light and strategic views to and from the interior. A large skylight brings natural light into the interior, becoming more diffuse as it passes down the stairwell.

| Project Name **Unterkrumbach Süd Bus Stop** | Location **Krumbach, Austria** |
| Architect / Designer **Architecten de Vylder Vinck Taillieu** | Date **2014** |

Influenced by a drawing by artist Sol LeWitt, and by the steep and jagged profile of the nearby Alpine mountains, this bus stop by Architecten de Vylder Vinck Taillieu is made from a four-sided folded, painted steel form, welded together with the assistance of skilled local craftspeople. One of seven architect-designed bus stops commissioned for the village of Krumbach, the project Unterkrumbach Süd, also called 'April', is a striking triangulated shelter that rests on two planes and a single point. The folded planes of the deep V-shaped form provide views out to oncoming transport but also protects waiting passengers from the elements.

 *Home within Home ...* by Do Ho Suh is an illuminating comment on the geographical, cultural and physical contrasts between the artist's birthplace in Korea and his life in the USA. The work renders a full-scale replica of a three-storey American townhouse in which he once lived, with a spectre of his family's traditional Korean home suspended inside. Both houses are meticulously made from a filmy blue fabric, articulated by a metal frame. This immediately describes the different size, structure and details specific to each place: the capacious mansard-roofed home engulfs the Hanok style house but both are rendered ghostly by the translucent blue mesh.

Project Name **Makoko Floating School**	Location **Lagos, Nigeria (or elsewhere)**
Architect / Designer **NLÉ**	Date **2014**

Faced with the challenges for coastal Africa caused by increasing urbanization and climate change, this three-storey floating school is a prototype for Makoko, a slum district in Lagos that is largely built on stilts and regularly suffers flooding. Built by local people and designed from readily available building materials, such as offcut timber from the saw mill and bamboo, the school can accommodate up to 100 adults. Its A-frame structure has a low centre of gravity that stabilizes and balances the boat, and is organized into three levels: a play area at the widest, lowest level; school rooms above; and workshops at the top. Though primarily designed for schooling, it can also accommodate other needs the community may have for events, clinics or a market.

Project Name	Sealight Pavilion	Location	Melbourne, Victoria, Australia
Architect / Designer	Monash Universty Department of Architecture	Date	2011

 Constructed from reclaimed cypress wood, this pair of waterside pavilions in Melbourne's revitalised Docklands was designed by architecture students at Monash University with architects Rintala Eggertsson, Grimshaw and Felicetti. The intention was to create a space that would amplify the natural phenomena of sea and sky, and also provide a place for the public to meet or shelter from the elements. Each pavilion is enclosed by a slatted timber facade that gradually becomes more open as the pavilions reach towards the sky or sea edge. Constructed in just over three months, the permanent pavilions weather and gain patina over time, becoming increasingly cohesive with their surroundings and well used.

This unusual cinema was created as part of the European Capital of Culture celebrations for the city of Guimarães. The structure capitalized on the use of cork - which is famously produced in Portugal. Its pale skin and dark interiors are both made of this popular material. Conceived in recognition of the 1950s CineClube, the Open Cinema was used to screen an hour-long film comprised of three-minute trailers. Viewers entered the cinema via sixteen funnels made of lemon-yellow painted steel, each accommodating several people. As clusters of viewers took in the screen, their multi-legged appearance from afar gave rise to the cinema's moniker, 'Centipede'.

Project Name **Tree Snake Houses**	Location **Pedras Salgadas Park, Portugal**
Architect / Designer **Luís and Tiago Rebelo de Andrade**	Date **2013**

 Designed as luxury ecological retreats in the ancient grounds of the Pedras Salgadas Spa and Nature Park, the Tree Snake Houses provide bespoke hotel accommodation while also provoking playful memories of being in a tree house. Cantilevered from a sloping site and held aloft by two pairs of steel supports, the houses appear to be shaped like snakes gliding between the surrounding trees. Clad in slate shingles and timber, the natural materials provide a degree of camouflage in the forested environment. Each house contains a bathroom, kitchen and bed set in front of a large picture window at the uppermost point.

| Project Name **Reuss Delta Tower** | Location **Reuss Delta, Switzerland** |
| Architect / Designer **Gion A. Caminada** | Date **2012** |

This lookout tower was commissioned to provide views for visitors to the Reuss Delta, a natural environment in central Switzerland known for its alpine peaks and large lakes. Enclosed by forty-eight trunks of silver fir, the tower's substantial timber columns are interspersed with four viewing platforms that are partially protected from the elements by an overhanging circular wooden roof with scalloped edges. Visitors access the tower via a suspended timber staircase that spirals around the central column and is enclosed by balustrades woven from cane, a technique that is also applied to the platforms and was made in collaboration with local artisans.

| Project Name **Tea Rooms** | Location **Jinhua, Zhejiang, China** |
| Architect / Designer **Jiakun Architects** | Date **2006** |

 These tearooms by Jiakun Architects are one of sixteen pavilions designed by different architects, each selected by artist Ai Weiwei. They form part of a 2 kilometre (1½ mi) long park along the Yiwu River near Shanghai built in commemoration of the artist's father, the poet Ai Qing. Raised up from the ground by a single steel post, each of the six tearooms is built of a simple steel-framed cube clad on two sides by semi-opaque glass and accessed by a narrow steel staircase. A three-sided section of aluminium alloy sits above the main structure and forms operable roof and walls. Visitors can manipulate the pulley mechanism to open or close the wing-like walls, creating either a protected enclosed private space, or a pavilion open to wind, sky and landscape.

 Part of Sydney's annual Sculpture by the Sea event, the House of Mirrors is formed from a large cube of gabion cages that defies the usual weighty use of these rock-filled structural vessels. In contrast, they are used here as an ephemeral structure with which to frame views of Sydney's coastline and are embedded with sheets of mirror-finished steel. An opening in each of the cube's six sides allows reflections of the rocks, sky, sea and lawn to reach the mirrored surfaces, creating a kaleidoscopic landscape that offers an unusual juxtaposition of natural elements surrounding the sculpture.

| Project Name **Isin Chapel** | Location **Istanbul, Turkey** | Date **2011** |

Architect / Designer **Breathnach, Donnellan, O'Brien with MEDS**

Perched on a steep cliff in Istanbul, this non-denominational chapel was envisaged as a place for repose by the sea, designed and built by Breathnach, Donnellan, O'Brien and their team of Meeting of Design Students (MEDS), which holds an annual European workshop. Informed by the theme, 'Bridging Cultures' and the intimate typology of Turkish mosques, the chapel is clad in oriented strand board (OSB) with wooden planks screening the lower half of the structure. The screens filter daylight into the lowered floor level that faces a spectacular view and is intended for meditation and reflection. Though the building itself is modest, its elevated position acts as a distinct beacon from afar.

| Project Name **Korkeasaari Lookout Tower** | Location **Helsinki, Finland** |
| Architect / Designer **Ville Hara** | Date **2002** |

This latticed timber structure stands 10 metres (32¾ ft) high on a point of Helsinki's Korkeasaari Island and is the winner of a student competition for a tower run by the Korkeasaari Zoo. Built from seventy-two long wooden battens that wrap around the tower's two platforms and staircases, each piece of curved timber was steamed on site and twisted into one of seven pre-bent forms, drawing on traditional boat building techniques. Held together with over 600 bolted joints, the load-bearing structure is made weather and UV resistant by a treatment of oil-based wood balm.

 Rem Koolhaas, the founding partner of OMA, was the seventh architect nominated to design the Serpentine Pavilion and, with structural designer Cecil Balmond, he literally lifted the roof of the pavilion. Based on a circular plan enclosed with tall translucent panels, the helium-filled translucent canopy was the crowning glory of the pavilion. Controlled by cables, its giant inflated roof rose and fell depending on the weather, tethered close to the crown on windy days and extending to its full height when sunny. The balloon often stood taller than the Serpentine Gallery and acted as a beacon for the temporary space, which was used to host talks, film screenings and two twenty-four-hour interview marathons.

In contrast to the historic surroundings of the Plaça de la Merce, this inflatable blue hand was commissioned as part of the BCN re.set pavilion series in Barcelona. It serves as a vibrant canopy that provides shade and acts as a marker for the civil wedding ceremonies celebrated beneath it. Marking recent changes that legally recognize interfaith, non-religious and same-sex marriages, Take My Hand hovers benevolently above a processional pathway and stage, giving shaded relief from strong sunshine in the plaza. The inflatable PVC installation is tethered to surrounding buildings and secured by concrete weights that stabilize it against wind or rain. Coloured a brilliant cornflower blue, the outstretched hand references the universal symbol for human rights and its fundamental aims.

| Project Name **St-Loup Chapel** | Location **Pompales, Switzerland** |
| Architect / Designer **LOCALARCHITECTURE with Danilo Mondada** | Date **2008** |

This demountable chapel was designed as a temporary home for the Deaconess Community of St-Loup to use while their historic premises were renovated. The project is predominantly constructed of 60 millimetre (2¼ in) deep timber panels that zig-zag in and out along its length, like an accordion. In collaboration with the IBOIS Institute at the EPFL, computerized software was used to determine the best dimensions and structural efficacy for each panel, which were quickly cut, then assembled on site. Deferring to the traditional distinction in width and height of the transept and nave, the chapel is organized with a wide horizontal entrance that rises and becomes narrower on approach to the altar. Polycarbonate panels fill the gabled ends and filter daylight into the interior.

Framed by a rectangular steel shell, this education centre for the Wild Reindeer Foundation charity is on the outskirts of Norway's Dovrefjell National Park, the home of Europe's last wild reindeer herds. The pavilion's 13.5 metre (44¼ ft) long glazed facade looks out to the Snøhetta mountain massif. Visitors can take in the view and watch wildlife roam from an undulating interior surface made of 250 square milimetres (9¾ sq in) pine beams, which form the tiered seating, entrance and distinctive roadside facade. Constructed by Norwegian shipbuilders, who milled and pegged together the curvaceous timber panels, the 90 square metre (295¼ sq ft) pavilion stands out from the grey and stony landscape.

| Project Name **Woods of Net** | Location **Kanagawa, Japan** |
| Architect / Designer **Tezuka Architects** | Date **2009** |

Like a gigantic interlocking wooden nest that encloses an enormous colourful net, this permeable children's playground is part of the Hakone Open-Air Museum in Japan. A collaboration between artist Toshiko Horiuchi MacAdam, and Tezuka Architects, Woods of Net is a semi-enclosed space for children to climb, swing and jump inside the rainbow of hand-knitted netting. Bulbous and webbed surfaces are suspended from the overarching timber frame, which was designed and built using traditional Japanese construction methods found in the temples of Nara and Kyoto. Requiring 320 cubic metres (1050 cu ft) of timber, each of the 589 structural members is unique in size and secured solely by the intricate system of joints.

Project Name **Sol Duc Cabin**		Location **Olympic National Park, Washington, USA**
Architect / Designer **Tom Kundig**		Date **2011**

The exterior sliding steel panel of this rural retreat on stilts is the consequence of the client's request for a 'virtually indestructible' home that could be locked up and left vacant for periods of time without being vandalized or flooded by the river nearby. The patina of the unfinished steel cladding and columns reflect the rugged natural environment and house a 30 square metre (98½ sq ft) space for the clients to stay during their fishing expeditions. Inside, the cabin has similarly raw finishes, with pale timber walls and floors, a partition of industrial steel mesh to the upper sleeping platform, and a balcony finished with the same mesh. On departure, the sliding doors and window shutters are simply wound closed to secure the cabin.

This prototype addresses Hong Kong's current housing crisis that means almost 7,200 people live cheek-by-jowl per square kilometre (18,000 per sq mi). The Bamboo Micro-Housing solution would provide temporary accommodation for the city's 280,000 impermanent dwellers. Constructed from the plentiful building material of bamboo, the 3 metre (9¾ ft) wide system of modular units includes all the basic features of a standard home and could be inserted and assembled inside disused factories. Held together with a custom-designed system of bolts and fasteners, and with enough room for a single inhabitant or a couple, the intent is to house communities of up to fifty micro-homes within one building.

| Project Name **The Nest** | Location **Bin Duong Province, Vietnam** |
| Architect / Designer **a21Studio** | Date **2013** |

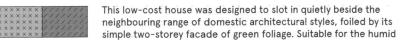

This low-cost house was designed to slot in quietly beside the neighbouring range of domestic architectural styles, foiled by its simple two-storey facade of green foliage. Suitable for the humid Vietnamese climate and the client's limited budget, the small home is marked by a gridded facade of white steel and mesh, which forms both fence and entrance and holds the potted plants. Composed of 900 × 900 millimetre (35½ × 35½ in) columns and 300 × 300 millimetre (11¾ × 11¾ in) beams the structure frames the open courtyard beyond, which leads to living, kitchen and dining spaces, with bed and bathrooms on the second level.

| Project Name | **Dovecote Studio** | Location | **Snape Maltings, England, UK** |
| Architect / Designer | **Haworth Tompkins** | Date | **2009** |

 Part of the Aldeburgh Music campus, a revered venue in the county of Suffolk, the Dovecote Studio provides a small studio for artists in residence, a rehearsal space for musicians or for the display of temporary exhibitions. The architects deferred to the overgrown vegetation and decaying brick form of the existing historic dovecote and instead inserted a prefabricated, welded Cor-Ten steel monocoque into the remains. Sympathetic to the red brick, the rusted steel gives way to an interior clad with plywood and divided into a lower level for performance/display and basic amenities, and an upper sleeping platform.

| Project Name **Kressbad Bus Stop** | Location **Krumbach, Austria** |
| Architect / Designer **Rintala Eggertsson Architects** | Date **2014** |

Located on a country road beside a tennis court, this bus shelter has a dual function, acting as bleachers for court spectators on one side, and as a bus stop for passengers on the other. Clad in pale wooden shingles, the project draws on the expertize of local timber craftsmanship to complete the shell, which has a stepped form and is arranged on two levels. On the ground floor the road-facing shelter has a simple full-width bench with a cutout window for passengers to watch for approaching transport. An internal staircase with darkened timber walls divides the lower bus stop from the upper level opposite and leads to the first floor, which houses seating for tennis enthusiasts.

Project Name	**Many Small Cubes**	Location	**Paris, France**
Architect / Designer	**Sou Fujimoto**	Date	**2014**

Recalling the flickering, shadowy experience of light cast beneath a tree's canopy, this installation, *Many Small Cubes*, by Sou Fujimoto stood in the midst of the Tuileries' tree-lined avenues in Paris. Commissioned by the Philippe Gravier gallery as one of a series of follies by noted architects and designers, the installation is formed of dozens of anodized aluminium boxes – some carrying potted trees – and each balanced in an apparently precarious way on a steel-framed structure. The stacked and cantilevered boxes are designed to form a central 'living space' void below, which is accessed from formal entries on each side – as well as from various small openings that daring visitors could squeeze through.

Part of 'Documenta 12', *Template* is an amalgam of 1,001 wooden doors and windows salvaged from Ming and Qing Dynasty houses that were demolished to make room for new development in China. Making a comment on China's industrial progress and the impermanence of its history, *Template's* door and window panels vary in texture, colour and size. The doors and windows range in age from 100 to 300 years old. Each is arranged in a grid to form eight panels that stand 4 metres (13 ft) high and extend from a central axis, secured by a wooden base. Because Ai Weiwei was unused to working with the strong weather conditions in Germany, the sculpture succumbed to Kassel's wind and rain; the inevitable collapse further underlined the artist's emphasis on the transience of all things.

INDEXES

INDEX OF MATERIALS

Terracotta
56

Brick
96, 245, 320

Mesh
234, 243, 316,
317

Velcro
47

Neon Tube
99

Plastic
17, 30, 44, 51, 85, 98, 106, 107,
109, 115, 117, 137, 140, 153, 155,
162, 164, 189, 218, 219, 223, 226,
227, 231, 235, 239, 241, 261, 267,
281, 285, 298, 303, 312, 313, 314

Elastic
35, 206, 211

Vinyl
98, 163, 296

Fibreglass
140, 174, 181,
237

Polyester
39, 45, 66, 90,
133, 154, 156,
222, 260, 302

Foam
68, 154, 221

Polyethylene
21, 156, 220

Cork
305

Sand
234

Cardboard
32, 46, 74, 113,
131, 192

Willow
18, 233

Leather
79

Copper Alloy
232

Brass
26

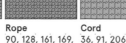

Timber
17, 19, 20, 23, 24, 25, 26, 27, 29, 30, 33, 35, 38, 40, 42, 43, 45, 48, 49, 50, 52, 53, 54, 55,
57, 59, 60, 63, 64, 65, 67, 70, 71, 72, 73, 75, 76, 77, 84, 86, 87, 89, 91, 92, 94, 95, 98, 100, 101,
105, 108, 109, 110, 111, 112, 114, 116, 118, 119, 120, 123, 124, 125, 126, 127, 129, 132, 133, 134, 135,
137, 138, 139, 140, 145, 146, 148, 149, 157, 158, 159, 160, 161, 164, 165, 166, 167, 169, 170, 171,
172, 173, 174, 175, 176, 177, 178, 179, 182, 183, 185, 186, 188, 189, 191, 192, 193, 194, 195, 198,
199, 201, 202, 203, 208, 209, 210, 214, 216, 217, 220, 221, 224, 226, 227, 228, 229, 231, 236,
237, 238, 239, 240, 241, 242, 243, 244, 245, 246, 247, 250, 251, 252, 253, 254, 255, 256,
257, 258, 259, 262, 263, 264, 267, 270, 271, 272, 273, 274, 275, 278, 279, 280, 282, 283, 286,
288, 289, 290, 292, 295, 297, 303, 304, 306, 307, 310, 311, 314, 315, 316, 317, 320, 321, 323

Corn Cobs	**Rope**	**Cord**	**Packing Tape**	**Bamboo**
86	90, 128, 161, 169,	36, 91, 206	142	205, 207, 259,
	190, 207, 222			278, 294, 303,
				318

Flax	**Cane**	**Plants**	**Sisal**	**Artificial Turf**
251	18, 307	164	91	91, 134, 141,
				209, 252

Glass	**ETFE**	**Wire**	**Aluminium**
62, 75, 108, 114, 116, 123, 126, 130,	284	64, 86, 136, 152,	36, 39, 41, 47,
144, 148, 166, 172, 196, 200, 201,		218, 309	51, 65, 68, 73,
204, 242, 246, 247, 252, 262,			78, 84, 102, 145,
263, 266, 270, 271, 282, 288, 293,			219, 223, 237,
308, 315, 317			257, 266, 299,
			308, 322

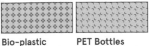

Bio-plastic
82, 93, 187

PET Bottles
230

Ice
64

Acrylic
24, 42, 92, 102,
103, 121, 134,
155, 157, 197

Tetra Pak
254

Mirror
28, 67, 97, 143,
168, 170, 257,
288, 309

Canvas
52, 53, 69, 243

Resin
166

Nylon
37, 103, 136,
152, 155, 297,
298

Polyurethane
16, 222

Fabric
21, 41, 47, 98,
162, 167, 218,
225, 258, 260

Acoustic Fabric
277

Plaster
40

Stone
236, 283

Iron
220

Carbon Fibre
166

Corrugated Iron
85, 160, 242,
265

Slate
306

Titanium
108

Stainless Steel
29, 67, 83, 86,
157, 226, 227,
276, 299

Cor-Ten Steel
159, 200, 204,
287, 320

Steel
18, 28, 31, 37, 52, 53, 55, 62, 69, 72, 85, 103, 110,
114, 115, 117, 121, 126, 137, 138, 153, 158, 159, 160, 162,
165, 166, 167, 168, 169, 170, 172, 175, 178, 180, 184,
185, 215, 224, 228, 229, 231, 232, 234, 238, 239,
246, 247, 252, 256, 262, 263, 265, 266, 267, 270,
277, 278, 279, 282, 284, 293, 295, 297, 298, 299,
300, 301, 305, 306, 308, 309, 312, 315, 317, 319, 322

Metal
26, 27, 79, 141,
147, 218, 285,
302, 319

Foil
131, 222

Rubber
37, 49, 88, 256,
297

Magnets
17, 225

Zinc
52, 157

Zinc Titanium
111

Asphalt
116, 272

Concrete
48, 54, 58, 63,
72, 75, 87, 122,
130, 144, 148,
172, 206, 209,
217, 232, 248,
249, 287, 291,
294, 299

Tissue
225

Paper
21, 22, 34, 104,
225, 283

INDEX OF ARCHITECTS, DESIGNERS, MAKERS, ARTISTS

0-to-1
108

A1 Architects
236, 283

A21Studio
319

Ábaton
244

Aberrant
Architecture
31

Achilles Design
167

Adjaye Associates
183

Affect-T
318

Ai WeiWei
323

Akihisa Hirata
Architecture Office
147

Alex Schweder
163

Allergutendinge
140

AllesWirdGut
87

Andreas Fuhrimann,
Gabrielle Hächler
Architekten
208

Andrew Kudless/
Matsys/Riyad Joucka
298

Angus Ritchie,
Daniel Tyler/
Processcraft
29

Anssi Lassila/
OOPEAA
149

António Martins,
Carlos Foyedo,
Luis Grilo
137

Appleton & Domingos
173

Architecten de
Vylder Vinck Taillieu
301

Architectural
Association School
of Architecture
33, 188

Architecture
Research Office
145

Architekturbüro
Scheder
262

ArchiWorkshop
115

Arnaud Huart
177

Arne Quinze
274

Asif Khan,
Pernilla Ohrstedt
284

Atelier565
288

Atelier Bow-Wow
76

Ateliers O-S
Architectes
131

Atelier Vecteur
119

Atelier Zündel
Cristea
223

Avatar Architettura
124, 241

Balestra Berlin
285

BaumRaum
126, 157

Behin Ha Design
Studio
164

Bergen School of
Architecture/OPA
FORM Architects
253

Breathnach,
Donnellan,
O'Brien/MEDS
310

Brenda Callander,
Jason Pielak, Stella
Cheung-Boyland
94

Broisson Architects
300

BSB Design
85

Buckminster Fuller
Institute/DRDesign/
ConformLab/
Goetz Composites/
Bruce Marek
197

Bureau A
54, 117

Bureau LADA
227

Cannatà & Fernandes
114

Carter Williamson
Architects
265

Casey Brown
Architecture
242

Charlie Whinney
Studio
73

Chun Qing Li/KREOD
133

Colin Fournier/
Marysia
Lewandowska/
NEON
305

Crosson Carnachan
Clarke
270

David Frazee/Broken
Arrow Workshop
62

Declan Burn,
Matt Ritani
49

Dedon
41

Design.Lab.
Workshop/
Brian Peters
107

Didier Faustino
96

Didzis Jaunzems
Architecture
277

dmvA
45

Do Ho Suh
302

Dorte Mandrup
Arkitekter
198

Dot Architects
16

Doug and Mike Starn
207

DRAA
273

dRMM Architects
228

DSDHA
280

DSH Architecture
36

DUS Architecten/
Studio for Unsolicited
Architecture
152

E/B Office
195

Ekkehard Altenburger
28

Emerging Objects
291

Emily Mannion,
Thomas O'Brien
251

Ensamble Studio
112, 144

Ernesto Neto
190

Esrawe + Cadena
184

Fabbricabois
35

FAM Architekti
282

Feilden Clegg Bradley
Studios
161

Formation
Association with
Edgar Arceneaux
95

Foster + Partners
276

Francesco Bombardi,
Simone Ardigò
61

Free Spirit Spheres
19

FriendsWithYou
297

Gabriel Lester
259

GAIA
21

Gartnerfuglen
Arkitekter
64

Gartnerfuglen/
Maria de Delás
243

Georgi Djongarski
47

Gion A. Caminada
307

Gitta Gschwendtner
71

H3T Architects
30

Hall McKnight
214

The Hanging Tent
Company
52

Hara Design Institute
22

Haugen Zohar
Arkitekter
139

Havel Ruck Projects
240

Haworth Tompkins
320

Heatherwick Studio
252

Hel Yes!
80

Hérault Arnod
Architectes
204

Herreros Arquitectos
160

Herzog & de Meuron
248

HHD_FUN
185

HOK
134

Ifat Finkelman,
Deborah
Warschawski
256

Innovation Imperative
20

Inrednin Gsgruppen
129

Instant Architects
230

IPT Architects
165

Jaanus Orgusaar
101

JAM Furniture
26

Javier Mariscal
74

Jeffery S. Poss
172

Jeppe Hein
78

Jerome W. Haferd,
K. Brandt Knapp
267

Jiakun Architects
308

Jiminez Lai
98

John Lin and Olivier
Ottevaere
189, 250, 292

John Locke/
Joaquin Reyes
156

Jonas Wagell
271

Jorge Gracia
159

Julio Barreno
Gutiérrez
215

Kacey Wong
79

Kalhöfer
Korschildgen
181

Kate Raudenbush
168

Kengo Kuma and
Associates
17, 146, 260

Kenya Hara
118

Klaas Kuiken
56

Korteknie
Stuhlmacher
Architecten
203

Kota Mizuishi
279

Krijn de Koning
105

LEAD/EDGE
Laboratory for
Architectural and
Urban Research
186

Lehrer Architects
141

Les Astronautes
221

LIKE Architects
88, 108, 131

Lily Jeon,
Diana, Koncan
103

Localarchitecture/
Danilo Mondada
314

London Fieldworks
70

London Fieldworks/
Malcolm Fraser
Architects
148

Lorcan O'Herlihy
Architects
180

Lucas Brown/
Green Mountain
College
120

Lucie Beauvert,
Paol Kemp with
Johanna Nocke
206

Luís and Tiago
Rebelo de Andrade
306

Manuel Villa
72

Marco Casagrande
233

Marco Hemmerling
102

Mark Reigelman and
Jenny Chapman
65

Marte.Marte
Architekten
200

Martin Azúa
66

Masakazu Shirane,
Saya Miyazaki
97

Massimo Uberti
99

Matthias
Loebermann
194

Max Rink,
Rachel Griffin,
Simon de Jong
216

Michael Jantzen
202, 255

Michiel van der Kley
93

Minsuk Cho
153

MMX
128

Modulorbeat
217, 232

Mojorno
176

Molo Studio
225

Monash University
Department of
Architecture/
Rintala Eggertsson/
Grimshaw/Felicetti
304

MOS Architects
90

Moskow Linn
Architects
237

MVRDV
25, 162

N55
239

NAS Architecture
170

Naumann
Architektur
111

Nendo
27

NEON
309

Nickisch Sano
Walder Architects
122

Nils Holger Moorman
182

Nixon Tulloch Fortey
89

NLÉ
303

Nott Architects
271

Numen/For Use
142, 222, 234

OBIKA Architecture
199

Observatorium
193

Office of McFarlane
Biggar Architects +
Designers Inc.
169

OH!SOM Architectes
246

Okamtoto Deguchi
Design
77

Olgga
201

OMA/Rem Koolhaas
312

OOF! Architecture/
Rose Nolan
245

Orproject
261

Overtreders W
220

PAD Studio/
Stephen Turner
174

Partisans
100

Patkau Architects
125

Paul Smith with
Nathalie de Leval
123

Penttinen Schönen
155

Peter Cook and Yael
Reisner
313

Peter Kunz
Architektur
130

PHTR Architects
138

Pier Alessio
Rizzardi/TCA Think
Tank
218

Pierre Stéphane
Dumas
44

Piet Hein Eek
175

Pieterjan Gijs,
Arnout Van
Vaerenbergh
287

Plastique
Fantastique/
IED Madrid
235

Poopy Cat
32

Porky Hefer
18

Productora
23

Raumlabor
281

RAW Design
68

RDAI
210

Renzo Piano
84

Riga Technical
University
254

Rintala Eggertsson
Architects
171, 278, 289, 321

RNL Architects
209

Rob Sweere
59, 296

Robbrecht en Daem
229

Robert Potokar and
Janez Breznik
42

Rodrigo Sheward
Giordano/University
of Talca
127

St André-Lang
Architectes
86

SandlellSandberg
38

Santambrogiomilano
196

Saunders
Architecture
55, 286

Sextafeira,
Produções
136

Smiljan Radić
75, 272

SmithlAllen Studio
82

Snøhetta
132, 315

Soma Architecture
219

SørenKorsgaard
43

Sou Fujimoto
179, 224, 322

Space International
91

Spacemakers
57

Spray Architecture
109

Standard
Architecture and
Design
63

Stefan Eberstadt
110

Stéphane Malka
263

Steve Messam
34

Studio Architecture/
Chris Chalmors/
Holmes-Culley
Engineers
192

Studio Chad Wright
48

Studio Makkink
and Bey
135, 247

Studio Dré Wapenaar
53

Studio MMASA,
Cipriano Chas
51

Studio Nomad
143

StudioMama
158

Supermachine Studio
249

T3arc
58

TAAT
290

Tadashi Kawamata
258

Talmon Biran
Architecture Studio
178

Terunobu Fujimori
40

Tezuka Architects
316

Tham and Videgård
Arkitekter
257

Thilo Frank
299

Tina Hovespian
46

Tom Fruin Studio
121

Tom Kundig
317

Tomás Saraceno
211

Tomokazu Hayakawa
Architects
238

Topotek 1
154

Toyo Ito
266

Uhlik Architekti
116

Ullmayer Sylvester
Architects
226

University of
Detmold, School of
Applied Science
191

University of
Manitoba
67

University of
Stuttgart ICD/ITKE
166, 187, 275, 295

Urban Nomads
37

Urbanus
205

Van Bo Le-Mentzel
24

Ville Hara
311

Vo Trong Nghia
Architects
294

Werner Tscholl
293

WMB Studio
69

White Arkitekter,
Happy,
Göteborgstryckeriet
104

Wilson Architects
264

Winfried Baumann
37

Worapong
Manupipatpong
50

Yong Ju Lee
83

Z-A Studio
113

Zebra3
92

ZO_loft Architecture
and Design
39

Ugandi 101
Jacob Shark 68
Jäger & Jäger 182
James Dow/Patkau
Architects 125
James Ewing/
Courtesy Public Art
Fund NY 78
Jan Kudej 116
Jason Havneraas/Unni
Skoglund 139
Jason Strauss 274
Jasper James,
Orproject 261
Javier Callejas Sevilla
160
Jeffery S. Poss 172
Jeremias Gonzalez
288
Jiakun Architects 308
Jin Boan 77
Joerg Hempel 181
John Locke 156
Jonathan Friedman
Photography/
Partisans 100
Joshua Holko 264
Joshua White
Photography 91
Judith Stichtenoth
228
Julio Barreno
Gutierrez 215
June Young Lim 115
Jusel Tlulnun 311
Kacey Wong 79
Kate Raudenbush 168
Katsuhisa Kida 316
Kieran Donnellan 310
Kilian O'Sullivan 226
Kiran Ridley 71
Klass Kuiken 56
Kristien Daem 229
Kuniaki Sasage 238
Laurent Clement 263
Lawrence Anderson
180
Leonie Schäfer 285
London Fieldworks
70, 148
Luca Berti 121
Lucia Degonda 307

Lucy Stoppele/
St André-Lang
Architectes 86
Luis Ferreira Alves 114
Luis Garcia 159
Luis Gordoa,
Gordoafotografia/
TuboHotel 58
Luke James Hayes 318
Manfred Richard
Hammer 187
Manuel Villa 72
Marc Domage 322
Marc Lins
Photography 200
Marco Cappelletti 218
Markus Bollen 126
Markus Marty and
Light Cave, co-
produced by the Art
Production Fund and
The Standard Hotels
297
Matthew Milman
Photography 291
Maya Virkus 262
Michael Jantzen 202,
255
Michel Denancé 210
Michiel van der Kley
93
Mila Hacke 194
Milo Keller 314
Molo Studio 225
MOS Architects 90
Moskow Linn
Architects 237
MVRDV 162
N55 239
Nathan Rist 62
Nic Granleese 245
Nicola Santini 124
Nicolas Waltefaugle
199
Nigel Ridgen 174
Nigel Young/Foster +
Partners 276
Nikita Wu 233
NLÉ 303
Nob Ruijgrok 175
Numen/For Use 222
Numen/For Use 234

OH!SOM Architectes
246
Olivier Helbig/Dedon
41
Olivier Ottevaere,
John Lin 189, 250, 292
OMB 169
Paol Kemp 206
Pasi Aalto 278
Paul Kozlowski 119
Paul Kozlowski/©
Photoarchitecture 170
Penny Clay 242
Pentinnen Schöne 155
Peter Clarke 89
Peter Lundström 38
Peter Lundstrom/
www.treehotel.se 129
Petr Krejci 123
Philip Vile 320
Pietro Savorelli 241
Poopy Cat 32
Porky Hefer 18
Poul Erik Korsgaard 43
Ralph Feiner 122
Ralph Kamena/
Courtesy Province
Zuid-Holland 247
Rasmus Norlander 104
Rei Niwa 17
Reinder Bakker 220
Ricardo Costa Oliveira
Martins Alves 306
Rintala Eggertsson
Architects 171
Rob Sweere/Thomas
Lenden 59, 296
Robert R. Roos 53
Robin Dupuis 221
Robin Hill 197
Rodrigo Sheward
Giordano/German
Valenzuela 127
Roger Wagner 87
Roland Halbe 144
Ross Campbell 29
Runze Hu 205
Sam Harnett/
wwwburnritani 49
Santambrogliomilano
196
Sergio Grazia 223

Sextafeira, Produções
136
Shin Inaba 97
Simon Devitt 270
Sina 290
SmithlAllen Studio 82
Spray Architecture
109
SPRIKK 216
Steve Messam 34
Studio Mariscal 74
Studio Thilo Frank 299
Studiomama 158
Studios Architecture
192
Takumi Ota 147
Tetra Shed® 20
Theo Simpson 67
Thierry Bal 193
Thomas Lenden 227
Thomas Randall-Page
254
Tim Bell 145
Tina Hovsepian 46
Tobias Balej 282
Toby Reed and Sam
Reed 138
Tom Chudleigh 19
Torben Eskerod 198
United Bottle Group
230
Valentin Jeck 130, 208
Valerie Bennett/
Architectural
Association 188
Veasyble Photo
Collection; photo
by Alessandra
Cinquemani 21
Winfried Baumann 37
Worapong
Manupipatpong 50
Yong Ju Lee 83
Yoshihiro Koitani 128
Zébra3 92
ZO_loft Architecture
and Design 39
Zooey Braun 111

Phaidon Press Limited
Regent's Wharf
All Saints Street
London N1 9PA

Phaidon Press Inc.
65 Bleecker Street
New York, NY10012

www.phaidon.com

First published 2016
© 2016 Phaidon Press Limited

ISBN 978 07148 7060 1

A CIP catalogue record for this book is
available from the British Library.

Commissioning Editor: Virginia McLeod
Project Editor: Rebecca Roke
Picture Research: Annalaura Palma
Production Controller: Steve Bryant

Design: StudioKanna

Printed in Romania